Jesus Said *It's Done*

(When Your Time Is Up)

REBECCA GRIFFIN

Copyright © 2024 Rebecca Griffin
All rights reserved
First Edition

PAGE PUBLISHING
Conneaut Lake, PA

First originally published by Page Publishing 2024

ISBN 978-1-6624-7827-7 (pbk)
ISBN 978-1-6624-7830-7 (digital)

Printed in the United States of America

This book is a special dedication to my beloved brother, Roger Griffin (Dre), who touched my life in so many ways. Although we had some challenging situations, God was always right there in the midst of them. During the process, we helped each other to recognize the errors of our thoughts and ways, which helped us to grow and mature spiritually. Although we were different, we had a lot in common. God put us closely together for a specific reason. It's our relationship that has inspired me to continue to do what God has called me to do. You left an indelible mark, and you will be forever embedded in my heart.

Rest well, my beloved.

Rebecca (Sis)

Contents

Foreword vii
Acknowledgments xi
Introduction xv

How the Title Came to Be 1
God's Timing 7
Dr. Tony Evans's Sermon: "The Rapture and the
    Church" 20
Will We Recognize Our Loved Ones? 27
The Mansion 30
The Book of Life and the Judgment Seat of Christ 34
Heaven and Hell 41
The Believer's Rewards 60
Dr. Tony Evans's Sermon: "It Is Finished" 69
It's Time to Make that Change 76
My Testimony 84
What the Word of God Says (Scriptures About Death) ... 86
What the Word of God Says (Comforting Scriptures) 89
Prayers (Comforting Prayers) 94

Poems (Thoughts and Expressions)

    To Our Beloved Dre 103
    Jesus Said It's Done 105

Irreplaceable 106
Gone but Not Forgotten 107
God Knows Best..108
Releasing You Back to God..................................109
My Heavenly Home 110
Jesus Set Me Free..111
Jesus Did It All for Me..112
God's Masterpiece 113

Bibliography...115

Foreword

Rebecca, I thank you for giving me around-the-clock access to your time, for your incredible energy, and for helping me and others during the bereavement period of our lives. Thanks for helping me to keep my eyes and heart focused on the prize, which is God. As I learn more and more about you, I know that God's plans are working in your life. Thanks to you and the powerful words of God. In your teaching, I will always be grateful and appreciative of you. May God continue to move forward with his plans for your life and this book. I pray that God will pour back into you all that you have poured out to me and others.

Missionary Lenell Hyman-Walker

I have known and been friends with the author of this book for over five years. I met Rebecca at Evangel Cathedral at a very difficult time in my life. We served together in several different ministries. Her service to the body of Christ has been in various capacities, as she has grown strong in faith and matured as a woman of God. It's been apparent to me and others that this woman has a passion for the word of God and serving others. Her life has been a living testament to that passion, and it's readily displayed in her relationship with her family and others. Her life exemplifies her dedication to serving and studying the word and serving the body of Christ, and her dedication continues until this day.

This no-nonsense woman is gifted and talented, and it's a privilege to know her. She is an awesome teacher, author, and prayer warrior. She is sincere, bold, and solid, and God is truly with her. The Epistle says in James 1:25 (KJV), "But whoso looked into the perfect law of liberty, and continued therein, he being not a forgetful hearer, but a doer of the work, this man shall be blessed indeed."

While dedicating herself, the author managed to further her profound belief in the word by expressing it through this dynamic inspirational book. *Jesus Said It's Done (When Your Time Is Up)* is a testimony of the author's life and her walk with God. Her words of encouragement were a blessing to me and my family during our time of bereavement, and I know this book will bless all who read it. It gives insight into what has driven her to dedicate her life to Christian servanthood. She was not only called to serve, but to do good works that are pleasing unto the Lord and to do it in the spirit of excellence.

> If anyone desires to come after Me, let Him deny himself, and take up his cross daily and follow Me. (Luke 9:23 NKJV)

I wholeheartedly recommend that you add this inspirational book to your Christian reading list, as it is truly a testament of a woman hearing God's calling and doing the work of our Lord Jesus Christ. The book speaks to life and death—from the comforting scriptures about death to comforting prayers and poems. You can see his mighty hand at work through the author. It is refreshing to see her love for the Lord and watch her continue to bathe herself daily in the word of God. I know this book was written by the inspiration of the Holy Spirit to encourage, motivate, and uplift those in need. I can hear the Father saying, "Well done, my good and faithful servant."

God bless you richly!

Rev. Dr. Joanne Butcher

Whether or not you're a believer and/or follower of Jesus Christ, at some point in your life, you'll experience good or bad conversations and/or situations that will be personal, professional, or political in context. There will be circumstances that will test your strength and mental capacity either physically and spiritually or both. For me, I seek a person of strong faith who has a relationship with Jesus Christ to either pray for me or with me. In this book, Rebecca arms you with all that you need with her poems and prayers to cover and prepare you with words that may not come easy to you with pure grace and elegance. This book will touch your heart and spirit, confirming unequivocally that God has anointed her with a wonderful gift to be shared.

Mary Rushdan, a friend and neighbor

Acknowledgments

This is to an awesome God who has always believed in me when I didn't believe in myself. To God, who has given me everything that I need to make this all happen. To God, who has showered me with his love, grace, mercy, blessing, and favor even when I didn't deserve it. From the rising of the sun until the going down of the same, I will continually bless your name and give you all the honor, glory, and praise.

The word of God says in 2 Timothy 2:15 (KJV), "Study to show yourself approved unto God, a workman that need not be ashamed, rightfully dividing the word of truth." I want to take this opportunity to honor and give thanks to an anointed and blessed man of God, Pastor Kevin R. Matthews for teaching (class: Studying the Bible for Yourself) me how to study the Bible for myself. Pastor Kevin, it's through your preaching and teaching that has helped me to discover my real true identity: who I am, whose I am, and what I have in Christ Jesus.

To Juliette, who rang my doorbell on a Friday night and told me that God had put it in her spirit to come and see me. She told me that she was praying for me, and then she asked me did anyone in my family had cancer. And I said yes. I never shared with her that my brother had cancer. God is so awesome, and he is still showing us signs, wonders, miracles, and revelations. I was truly blessed by her obedience and willingness to do what God had asked her to do.

To my family whom I love dearly. I thank God for each one of you, and for being an integral part of my life and heart. I pray that God will continue to watch over you, show you how much he loves you, and strengthen, instruct, and teach you in the way that you should go. I pray that God will shower them with his tender mercies and grace.

I want to thank Conductor Rose, Conductor Paul, and all the Gospel Train Prayer Line riders, for the love that that they have shown me since I boarded the train. I thank the leaders of the prayer line, Conductor Rose and Conductor Paul, for allowing me to use the gifts that God has blessed and given to me, so that I can be a blessing to someone else. I thank God for the awesome men and women who board the train and how their teaching, preaching, praying, and testimonies have enriched my life spiritually. God bless each one of you exceedingly and abundantly above all that you can think of or ask for.

This is to all those who helped me along the way. I thank you for helping me to carry my burdens, for praying for me and my family, for your words of encouragement, and for uplifting and inspiring me during Roger's and my times of sickness, pain, sorrow, trials, and tribulations. I pray that the God that we serve will pour back into you all that you have poured out to us; and that the Lord's recompense toward you and your family will be greater than what you can ever imagine. Let our God be glorified, his people be edified, and the devil be horrified. I pray that this day and all your days will be filled with God's Spirit, his love, his peace, his joy, his strength, his grace, his tender mercies, and most importantly his word.

Introduction

Before my brother's funeral, I asked God to help me to write a poem to my brother, and God woke up the gift that was lying dormant in me, and he showed me how to use it. Glory to God! Over the years I have been encouraged by others to write, and it took the death of my beloved brother to start the process. My study and meditation of God's word, along with the people that he has put in my life, are helping me to deal with my grieving. The information contained therein goes beyond the grieving process. In March 1995, my father died in my presence. I was devastated, and I grieved for a long time.

At that time I was not saved, and I was spiritually naive about what the Bible says about all the good things that Jesus had done for me and what I needed to do to have an abundant life on earth and eternal life with him. I didn't know about what happens to the body when we die and what to expect in the afterlife on this earth. A lot of people don't like talking about death, but the reality is it's a part of life. They don't know what to expect or look forward to when that time comes. If you are saddened by someone whose death is imminent, or grieving because of the loss of your loved one, I pray that you will find comfort and solace in what is contained in this book.

How the Title Came to Be

For various reasons, as a young girl (the oldest), I had the responsibility of taking care of my brothers (six), along with my other daily chores. This responsibility was mine until I graduated from high school. At that time, I never got to experience life outside what I was confined to do at home. Prior to 2019, my mother took care of her son, and then she became ill and couldn't do it anymore. He was placed in a group home, which was a two-hour drive from where the family lived. There were times when I told God that I didn't want that cup. He reminded me that he had already prepared and equipped me for such a time as this. After forty-two years of working for the federal government, I retired, and I wanted to start living instead of existing. Although I wanted to do otherwise, God's calling in my life superseded what I wanted to do, which is to serve others, especially those who are in need and those who are sick, weak, and afflicted.

I was not only called to serve, but to do good works that are pleasing unto the Lord and to do it in the spirit of excellence. He also reminded me of Luke 9:23 (NKJV), "If anyone desires to come after Me, let him deny himself, and take up his cross daily and follow Me." Every day, I thought about my brother and prayed for his well-being and those who were responsible for taking care of him.

I was determined to see my brother, so I asked an awesome woman of God to take me. And she was more than glad to do it. I tried to be strong and not cry, and when I saw him, I held him as tight as I could. He always called me Sis, and he said, "What are you crying for?" I was appalled at the condition of the group home, the lack of care my brother was getting. He was left alone, and he was shaking like a leaf on a tree. We spent some quality time with him. I was determined to take him out of that nasty group home, and I told him that I was coming back to get him. I made arrangements the following week, and I brought my brother back to live with me. More than forty years later, I found myself reliving and tasked with the same responsibility, nurturing and taking care of my beloved brother.

In June 2019, I became the caregiver and representative for my brother, Roger, affectionately known as Dre. He was diagnosed with dementia. One morning, I called him down for breakfast, and he was unable to walk down the steps. I had him scoot down the steps, and when he got to the bottom step, he could barely stand up or walk. I was calling and crying out to Jesus to help me to get him up off the floor to the sofa. Of course, he showed up. I got Dre ready and took him to the hospital. After several days of being in the hospital, the doctor recommended that he be sent to a nursing home for rehabilitation. Because of the lack of support, it was beginning to be too much for me. In addition, I became sick. I had a procedure done on both legs and a bone fusion in my upper spine. In January

2021, I requested an application for long-term care from the nursing home. Shortly thereafter, he was approved by the state for long-term care.

Because of the coronavirus, the nursing home wasn't allowing family and friends to visit their loved ones. In July 2021, the nursing home opened its doors for visitation. On July 6, 2021, my brother Joseph and I began visiting our brother at the nursing home. He appeared to be upbeat. He was laughing and talking. Then two weeks later, we went to see him, and things began to change drastically. His stomach was swollen. He was not as responsive. His voice became raspy, and later on, he was experiencing breathing problems. I had to go to the nursing home and insist that the nurse call the ambulance to transport my brother to the hospital. Shortly after being in the hospital, he was diagnosed with masses on his liver, and the doctor informed me to take him to see an oncologist.

On September 20, 2021, Joseph and I took him to see the oncologist, and the doctor informed us that no medication or operation could help him at this point. He was close to his fourth stage of cancer, and she recommended that he receive hospice care. After the doctor gave us the news, Joseph and I broke down and cried. Dre never shed one tear. After we left the doctor's office, Joseph went to get the car while Dre and I waited on the sidewalk. He was in a wheelchair, but he could barely sit up straight. He kept leaning to the side. As I was standing beside him, I told him to lay his head on me, and these are the last words I heard my brother say: "Jesus said it's done."

I heard him the first time, and I asked him again, "What did you say?"

And he said, "Jesus said it's done."

I began to cry more and more, and as people were walking by, they came over to comfort and minister to me. When we took him back to the nursing home, there was a caregiver standing outside who had come to the nursing home to visit someone else, and I was still crying while Joseph was trying to take him out of the car. The caregiver assisted my brother in getting Dre out of the car into the wheelchair, and my tears were steadily flowing. She called me to the side and told me to release him back to God, and to set aside my selfish reason for wanting him to stay due to his severe condition.

On September 24, 2021, I met with the hospice coordinator and signed a consent form to give them permission to go to the nursing home to provide care for him. Shortly after meeting with the hospice coordinator, I received a telephone call informing the family to start making funeral arrangements. Unfortunately, the nursing home had a terrible outbreak of coronavirus, and the family wasn't able to visit Dre during his final days of transition. I wanted so much to be with him, but I know for sure that God was there because he is omnipresent.

On October 18, 2021, God called our beloved brother home. It was like God had already given him a revelation that his death was imminent, and he accepted it. Whatever calling God had on his life was over, and his labor of work on this earth was completed. Due to dementia and other illnesses, he suffered for a while, so God brought his suffering and pain to an end. When Dre said, "Jesus said it's done," it brought back to my remembrance the sixth statement Jesus said while he was dying on the cross, "It is finished."

The sixth statement let us know that his suffering was over, and the task that the Heavenly Father had assigned to him was completed. In his obedience to the Father, he gave his love for mankind by paying the death penalty for our sins so that we could be redeemed and be reconciled back to the Father. The sixth statement is discussed in more detail in another section of this book.

In keeping it real, there were times when I wanted to give up. Sometimes I wanted to run away, but I know I can't run away or hide from God. Sometimes I felt faithless and hopeless, but God always intervened on my behalf. And he always brought me back to where he wanted me to be: closer to him. During those tumultuous times even when I didn't want to do anything, I was still praising and thanking God for all the good things that he has done. I continued to take care of Dre and myself, as well as my mother and my household. I was still ministering and helping others and teaching on the Gospel Train Prayer Line. I couldn't have done all these things without God; he will always be my source, and he will supply the resources.

During those times, I was reading various Scriptures that applied to our situations and circumstances. I was given a scripture to read and to memorize:

> It shall come to pass in that day. That his burden will be taken away from your shoulder. And his yoke from your neck.

> And the yoke will be destroyed because of
> the anointing oil. (Isaiah 10:27 NKJV)

This was a grievous yoke, and it had become a burden to us. The words *yoke* and *burden* are synonymous with carrying a heavy load. Seeing the state that my brother was in brought on many heartaches and tears, and I was close to the point of having a nervous breakdown. I was praying for a physical healing, but because God's ways and thoughts are higher than mine (and yours), he did what he knew was best for the both of us. Whatever we are faced with in this life, God's will is going to be done (let your will be done on earth as it is in heaven). Amen. Let it be so. We both were delivered from our burdens. The yoke shall not only be taken away, but it *shall be destroyed.* The enemy shall no more recover his strength to do the mischief he has done, and this is *because of the anointing* for their sakes who were partakers of the anointing. For the sake of the Messiah, the Anointed of God, whom God had an eye to in all the deliverances of the Old Testament church and had still an eye to in all the favors he shows to his people, it is for his sake that the yoke is broken and that we are made free indeed.[1] The scripture said in John 8:36 (NKJV): "Therefore if the Son (Jesus) makes you free, you shall be free indeed."

To God be all the glory for all the good things he has done!

---

[1] Matthew Henry's *Commentary on the Whole Bible.* New Modern Edition, complete and unabridged in six volumes. Ninth Edition (2009). Peabody, Massachusetts. Hendrickson Publishers Inc. (1991). *Isaiah to Malachi*, volume 4 of 6 volumes, pp. 56. The burden will be lifted, and the yoke will be taken away.

God's Timing

Time is something that we deal with every day, and it's something that everyone thinks they understand. Time has many aspects and represents different things to people in different circumstances. The word *time* is defined as a period during which an action, process, or condition exists or continues. It's also a point or period when something occurs—for example, a moment, hour, day, or year. The Bible speaks of a set or appointed time, a period and divisions of time (day, week, month, and year). Time is one of our greatest commodities, and we often take it for granted. God didn't create time for himself because he exists outside and beyond time and space. God says in Revelation 22:13 (NKJV), "I am the Alpha and the Omega, the beginning and the end, the first and the last." Now what does the word of God say about time? It says in the book of Ecclesiastes 3:1–8 (NKJV):

> To everything there is a season,
> A time for every purpose under heaven.
> A time to be born, and a time to die.
> A time to plant, and a time to pluck what
>   is planted.
> A time to kill, and a time to heal.

> A time to break down, and a time to build up.
> A time to weep, and a time to laugh.
> A time to mourn, and a time to dance.
> A time to cast away stones, and a time to gather stones.
> A time to embrace, and a time to refrain from embracing.
> A time to gain, and a time to lose.
> A time to keep, and a time to throw away.
> A time to tear, and a time to sew.
> A time to keep silence, and a time to speak.
> A time to love, and a time to hate.
> A time of war, and a time of peace.

We are told in the first verse: "To everything there is a season, a time for every purpose under heaven." You see, folks got it twisted. God's timing isn't our timing, and our timing is not his timing. It is God who puts everything into a specific order or relation—even the tiniest details of our surroundings. His timetable is perfect (Why?) because he is perfect and he is an on-time God. Yes, he is. The Bible tells us that certain events were ordained (meant to happen) before the foundation of the earth. All the events in our lives do not randomly happen by chance. Nothing God does is happenstance or accidental, and he has a plan and a purpose for everything he does. Every purpose has its time.

When it comes to our God-ordained purpose and destiny, it has already been etched in stone. You cannot erase, alter, or say that it doesn't exist. No matter what we attempt to do or how hard we try, we can't change the purpose and destiny that God has ordained for our life. The scope of these verses is to show that we live in a world of changes and that several events of time and conditions of human life are vastly different from one another and yet occur promiscuously, and we are continually passing and repassing between them as in revolutions of every day and every year. Every change concerning us, with time and season of it, is unalterably fixed and determined by a supreme power; and we must take things as they come, for it is not in our power to change what is appointed for us. Some of these changes are purely the act of God, and others depend more upon the will of man, but all are determined by the divine counsel. Everything under heaven (earth) is changeable, but in heaven they are unchangeable. And God is unchangeable concerning these things.[2] God does not change and he will never change. He is immutable. Jesus Christ is the same yesterday, today, and forever (Hebrews 13:8 NKJV).

> For I am the LORD, I do not change.
> (Malachi 3:6 NKJV)

His name is called Elohim (means strong and powerful creator). See the book of Genesis chapters 1 and 2. He created the first man and woman, Adam and Eve. These two human beings were not conceived in, or came from the womb of a woman.

---

[2] Ibid., *Job to Song of Solomon*, volume 3 of 6 volumes, pp. 819. Everything on earth is changeable, but in heaven they are unchangeable.

It says in Genesis 1:27 (NKJV), "So God created man in his own image, in the image of God he created him, male and female he created them."

And then God did this in Genesis 2:7 (NKJV), "And the Lord God formed man of the dust of the ground, and breathed into his nostrils the breath of life, and man became a living being."

Then he said in Genesis 2:18 (NKJV), "And the Lord God said, 'It is not good that man should be alone. I will make him a helper comparable to him.'"

This is what he did in Genesis 2:21–23 (NKJV), "And the Lord God caused a deep sleep to fall on Adam, and he slept; and he took one of his ribs, and closed up the flesh in its place. Then the rib which the Lord God had taken from man he made into a woman, and he brought her to the man. And Adam said, 'This is now bone of my bones, and flesh of my flesh; she shall be called woman, because she was taken out of man.'"

Adam did this in Genesis 3:20 (NKJV), "Adam called his wife's name Eve, because she was the mother of all living."

There is a time to be born and a time to die. These are determined by the divine counsel. As there is *a time to be born and a time to die*, so there will be a time to rise again, a set time when those who lie in the grave shall be remembered.[3] It says in Job 14:13 (NKJV), "Oh, that you would hide me in the grave that you would conceal me until your wrath is past, that you would appoint me a set time, and remember me!"

---

[3] Ibid., *Job to Song of Solomon*, volume 3 of 6 volumes, pp. 819. A time to be born, a time to die, and a time to rise.

The Bible says, "There is a time to be born." God was thinking about us long before we ever thought about him. Our life predates our conception. Before we were conceived in our mother's womb, he thought about us and planned it before we existed and without our input.

> Know that the LORD, he is God. It is He who has made us and not we ourselves. We are his people and the sheep of his pasture. (Psalm 100:3 NKJV)

God is the creator of all living things. That's what makes each one of us unique in his eyes. We are his workmanship and his masterpiece. He is the one who appoints your birthday (the day, date, and year) you are born. We have no control over whom we are born to: our gender, our ethnicity, the way we look, whether we are short or tall, or born wealthy or poor. All things are destined of God. We can choose our friends, careers, cars, spouses, hobbies, and clothes, etc., but we cannot choose whom God has created us to be.

He is omniscient an all-wise and all-knowing God, and he knows everything about you. We are reminded in Psalm 139 (NIV) how well God knows us. He knows what you are going to do, how you are going to do it, when you are going to do it, and where you are going to do it. He knows what you are thinking before you think it. He knows what you are going to say before you say it. He knows all about your secrets and your sins. He knows when you come and go. He knows when you sit and when you rise. He knows all about your needs and desires. And he is familiar with all your ways. Nothing is ever hidden from God.

He is also called El Roi (the God who sees). Although he sits on his throne high up in the heavens at the right hand of his Father, he sees you no matter where you are. He is not a distant God, and he does not isolate himself from those he loves. He doesn't need binoculars to see you, or a Global Positioning System (GPS) to track you.

> For his eyes are on the ways of man.
> And he sees all his steps. (Job 34:21 NKJV)

There are a lot of questions about death. For example, what happens to the spirit, soul, and body? Does our consciousness continue, or do we just sleep awaiting the Second Coming of Jesus Christ and the final judgment? What happens between death and resurrection? Is there life after death? What will our new body look like? Will we recognize our loved ones? All our days on this earth are numbered. Death will come to all of us eventually—sometimes suddenly with little or no warning, other times at the end of a long and serious illness. The end of verse 2 says, "And a time to die."

What happens when we die? All human beings are made up of three parts: the body, soul, and spirit. We live in the body. We have a soul and a spirit, which make up the whole of you. The spirit and soul cannot be destroyed. When death comes, there is a separation of the body, the soul, and the spirit. The body is the outer covering, and it is only the temporary residence of humans. When we die, the body will return to dust. It says in Genesis 3:19 (NKJV), "In the sweat of your face you will eat your bread until you return to the ground, for out of it you were taken; for dust you are and to dust you will return."

And in Psalm 104:29 (NKJV), "You take away their breath, they die and return to their dust." The soul goes immediately into the presence the Lord.

Those who believe in God's word are looking forward to the day when they will live in his presence. Paul says in 2 Corinthians 5:6–9 (NKJV), "So we are always confident knowing that while we are at home in the body we are absent from the Lord. For we walk by faith and not by sight. We are confident, yes, well pleased rather than to be absent from the body and to be present with the Lord. Therefore we make it our aim, whether present or absent to be well pleasing to him."

Knowing that he would be with the Lord, the apostle Paul looked at his own death as a gain. He says in Philippians 1:21–23 (NKJV), "For to me, to live is Christ, and to die is gain. But if I live on in the flesh, this will mean fruit from my labor; yet what I shall choose I cannot tell. For I am hard pressed between the two, having a desire to depart and be with Christ which is far better."

For those who are dying or have died, every believer who trusts in Jesus Christ will be safe and secure in his presence at the time of death and in the final resurrection of the body. We are reminded that this world we live in is not our home. We are just foreigners living in a strange land. God gives life, and he takes life because it belongs to him. He is a sovereign God, and there is nothing and no one who can take your life before your God-ordained days are finished. God is the one who can either lengthen or shorten your days on this earth. He has the final say so.

Death comes upon us in God's timing. Each one of us will experience death differently. For some, it may take minutes, days, or months to separate from the physical body. The body will go through some physical changes when death is near. The various signs may or may not apply to everyone. This is a brief summary of what I've learned about the signs. They may become disoriented. They may become talkative about the past, or not say too much at all. They don't have the desire to eat much. They may sleep a little more than usual. Their breathing becomes shallow. Their oxygen level decreases. Their energy and vital organs begin to shut down. Their skin color may change in some areas.[4]

On March 4, 1995, the nurse called the family to come to the hospital because our father wasn't doing too well. Once we arrived, he was lying there quietly, not saying too much. He had lost some weight, and his eyes looked very weak. Some of the family members visited for a while, and then they left. I stayed, and Dad began to lean to the side, and he looked uncomfortable. I asked him if he needed help, and he said yes. I attempted to assist him. I pushed the button for the nurse to come and help me. And it seemed like it took her forever. By that time, he was having difficulty breathing. When the nurse finally arrived, she said to me, "Your father is dying."

---

[4] Barbara Karnes. *Gone from My Sight (The Dying Experience)*. Vancouver, Washington (1986), revised 2020, pp. 1–13. Various signs of death, but they may or may not apply to everyone.

When I looked at him, the eyes that were once weak appeared to be bright. There was a glow in his eyes. In my tears and pain, I tried to pray. I called the family to give them the news.

There are two people mentioned in the Bible who never experienced death. The first person was a man named Enoch. It says in Genesis 5:21–24 (NIV), "When Enoch had lived 65 years, he became the father of Methuselah. And after he became the father of Methuselah, Enoch walked with God for 300 years, and had other sons and daughters. Altogether, Enoch lived 365 years. Enoch walked with God, and then he was no more, because God took him away." God was very pleased with him.

It says in Hebrews 11:5 NIV, "By faith Enoch was taken from this life, so that he did not experience death, he could not be found, because God had taken him away. Before he was taken, he was commended as one who pleased God."

The second person who didn't experience death is Elijah. He was a prophet in the Old Testament. He prophesied without fear and was a strong man of words and actions. He prophesied during the reigns of Ahab and Jezebel, Ahaziah, and Jehoram. It says in 2 Kings 2:11–12 (NIV), "As they (Elijah and Elisha) were walking along and talking together, suddenly a chariot of fire and horses of fire appeared and separated the two of them, and Elijah went up to heaven in a whirlwind. And Elisha saw him no more."

Enoch and Elijah did not experience what some of us are dreadful and fearful of—death.

The ungodly and profane are without God in the world; they walk contrary to him: but the godly walk with God, which presupposes reconciliation to God, for two *cannot walk together except they be agreed* (Amos 3:3), and includes all parts and instances of a godly, righteous, and sober life. To walk with God is to set God always before us and to act as those who are always under his eye. It is to live a life of communion with God both in ordinances and providences. It is to make God's word our rule and his glory our end in all our actions. It is to make it our constant care and endeavor in everything to please God and nothing to offend him. It is to comply with his will, to concur with his designs, and to be workers together with him. It is to be *followers of him as dear children*. He was entirely dead to this world and did not only walk after God, as all good men do, but he walked with God as if he were in heaven already. He lived above the rate, not only of other men but also of other saints, not only good in bad times but also the best in good times. Walking with God pleases God. We cannot walk with God unless we are walking by faith. God himself will put honor upon those who by faith walk with him so as to please him. He will own them now and witness for them before angels and men on the great day. Those who have not this testimony before the translation, you shall have it afterward. Those whose conversation in the world is truly holy shall find their removal out of it truly happy. Enoch's translation was not only evidence of faith in the reality of a future state and of the possibility of the body's existing in glory in that state, but it was also an encouragement to the hope of all that walk with God that they shall be forever with him: signal piety shall be crowned with signal honors.[5]

Elijah is carried up to heaven in a fiery chariot. Like Enoch, he was translated that he should not see death. It is not for us to say why God would put such a peculiar honor upon Elijah above any other of the prophets; he was a man *subject to like passions as we* are, knew sin, and yet never tasted death. Therefore is he dignified and thus distinguished as a man whom the King of kings did delight to honor? We may suppose that, herein, God looked back upon his past services, which were eminent and extraordinary, and intended a recompense for those and an encouragement to the sons of the prophets to tread in the steps of his zeal and faithfulness, and whatever it cost them, to witness against the corruption of the age they lived in. He looked down upon the present dark and degenerate state of the church and would give a very sensible proof of another life after this and draw the hearts of the faithful few upward toward himself and that other life. He looked forward to the evangelical dispensation and, in the translation of Elijah, gave a type and figure of the *ascension of Christ and opening of the kingdom of heaven to all believers*. Elijah had, by faith and prayer, conversed much with heaven, and now he is taken to that place to assure us that if we have our conversation in heaven while we are here on earth, we shall

---

[5] Matthew Henry's *Commentary on the Whole Bible*. New Modern Edition, complete and unabridged in six volumes. Ninth Edition (2009). Peabody, Massachusetts. Hendrickson Publishers Inc. (1991). *Genesis to Deuteronomy*, volume 1 of 6 volumes, pp. 40–41. Enoch was translated that he should not see death.

be there shortly; and the soul shall (and that is the man) be happy there forever.[6]

The word of God says this about faith in Hebrews 11:6 (NIV): "And without faith it is impossible to please God, because anyone who comes to him must believe that he exists and that he rewards those who earnestly seek him." It says in Hebrews 11:1 (NKJV), "Now faith is the substance of things hoped for, the evidence of things not seen." Hebrews 11:1 is further explained in Romans 8:24–25 (NKJV): "For we were saved in this hope, but hope that is seen is not hope, for why does one still hope for what he sees? But if we hope for what we do not see, we eagerly wait for it with perseverance."

Additional reading about the faith of God's Old Testament followers can be found in the book of Hebrews chapter 11. You can also go back to the Old Testament and read the stories about the faith of Abel, Noah, Abraham, Isaac, Jacob, Joseph, Moses, Rahab, Gideon, Barak, Samson, Jephthah, David, Samuel, and the other prophets.

In the New Testament, the faith Jesus is looking for is to have confidence and trust that God is able, through his Son (Jesus), to do what he has promised. It says in Mark 11:22–24 (NKJV),

> Have faith in God. For assuredly, I say to you, whoever says to this mountain be removed and be cast into the sea, and does not doubt in his heart, but believes

---

[6] Ibid., *Joshua to Esther*, volume 2 of 6 volumes, pp. 553–555. Elijah was translated that he should not see death.

that those things he says will be done, he will have whatever he says. Therefore I say to you, whatever things you ask when you pray believe that you receive them, and you will have them.

Great is God's faithfulness toward us.

Dr. Tony Evans's Sermon
"The Rapture and the Church"

Dr. Tony Evans is the founder and senior pastor of Oak Cliff Bible Fellowship Church, in Dallas, Texas. He is also the founder and president of the Urban Alternative, and the author of many books. Dr. Evans is the first African American to earn a doctorate of theology from Dallas Theological Seminary, as well as the first African American to author both a study Bible and full Bible commentary. His radio broadcast, *The Alternative with Dr. Tony Evans*, can be heard on more than one thousand outlets daily, and in more than one hundred and thirty countries. The following is his sermon titled "The Rapture and the Church." This sermon has helped me to get a better understanding of the rapture and how it works.

The next event on God's prophetic calendar is the rapture, and that is the next thing that is going to happen. The word *rapture* means to seize, grasp, or grab. It refers to Christ who is coming to retrieve his church (the believers), who has accepted him as their savior. Jesus told his disciples, "I'm leaving." He's getting ready to die on the cross, rise from the dead, and ascend back to heaven. He told them you cannot come with me now, and don't worry—I'm coming back to get you. When the disciples heard that they became dramatized, because for three years Jesus had been their teacher, provider, helper, leader, deliverer, and guide. He had been their whole world for three years. Jesus said in John 14:1–3 (NKJV), "Let not let your heart be troubled, you believe in God, believe also in me. In my Father's house are many mansions, if it were not so, I would have told you. I go to prepare a place for you. And if I go and prepare a place for you, I will come again and receive you unto myself that where I am there you may be also." This is the first specific reference to the rapture (I am coming to receive you back to me).

The apostle Paul gives us a detailed explanation for this event called the catching up or the rapture. He said in 1 Thessalonians 4:13 (NIV), "Brothers, we do want you to be ignorant about those who fall asleep, or to grieve like the rest of men who have no hope." He's telling you, don't be uninformed or unclear about those who are asleep. We would say those who have died. While they are waiting for him to come back, some of their loved ones died who are Christians, and they were concerned. If they are waiting for him to come back and some of our folks have died, will they miss his return because they are not alive like we are? The question here is who died, and are they missing out on this promise? One of the reasons why the apostle Paul discusses the rapture is to inform us about how this thing is going to work with people who are already dead. Another reason is because flesh and blood cannot inherit the kingdom of heaven. You can't go to heaven like you are now. You can't function like you are as flesh and blood, so a change has to occur.

Another reason why the rapture is important is to remove you before all hell breaks loose on earth. Paul said in 1 Thessalonians 1:10 (NIV), "And to wait for his Son from heaven, whom he raised from the dead, even Jesus who rescues us from the coming wrath." No matter how bad things are right now, you haven't seen nothing yet. When all hell breaks loose, it's called the tribulation. Before all hell breaks loose (the wrath that is to come), he is going to come to retrieve his people. There are a number of illustrations in the Bible. God retrieved Lot out of Sodom and Gomorrah before he rained down fire and brimstone. He retrieved Noah and his family into the ark before he flooded the world. He retrieved Rahab and her family before the walls of Jericho collapsed. God kept them from the judgment to come by retrieving them. That is the concept of the rapture, or the reasons for it.

He gives another reason why we need to know about the rapture, so that we don't grieve as those who have no hope. It can affect your emotional well-being. There are two kinds of grieving: hopeless grieving and hopeful grieving. Hopeful grieving is, *I am going to see this person again.* Both are grieving, but they are grieving differently. One is grieving without hope, and the other is grieving with hope. Don't be hopeless in your sorrow when you lose loved ones who are part of the family of God.

Paul introduces us to the word sleep, and he said in 1 Thessalonians 4:14 (NIV), "We believe that Jesus died and rose again; and so we believe that God will bring with Jesus those who have fallen asleep in him." We are talking about those who have fallen asleep, but then Jesus is bringing somebody with him when he comes. He's coming from heaven and the person that he's bringing are those who have fallen asleep. Wait a minute, the folks who have fallen asleep are in the grave, but the people he's bringing with him are the ones who have fallen asleep and coming with him from heaven. So which is it? I am in the grave, or I am in heaven?

When you expire, the life principle that God breaths in (soul) slithers in some visible way out of the body, and the body can no longer function because the soul has departed from it. The soul of the believer goes immediately into the presence of God. At the time of the rapture, when Jesus Christ descends to seize believers, he's coming with you. It's you that left when you went to sleep. When the Lord comes for the rapture of the saints, he says we who are alive. If he comes back in the next five minutes, everyone who is alive will have to take second place to those folks who have already died. We will not precede them. You are not going to beat them to heaven, even though they are dead (sleep), and you are alive. How is this is going to work? Verse 16 says the Lord himself will descend from heaven with a shout with the voice of an archangel, and with the trumpet of God, and the dead in Christ will rise first.

Now exactly what's rising? You are going to be buried, but not your soul, because it left at the point of death. When you are buried, most of us will be put in a casket and put under six feet of dirt. Others who died and don't get buried (died at sea, etc.) were not put in a casket—they were just buried in the ground. Therefore, in order to get your soul that's coming down into its new house to live in, there has to be a reconstruction of you. You have to be stitched back together again. You will be resurrected in some supernatural way, so your soul that is coming back with you has a place to hang out. The dead shall rise first—that's not your soul, but your body. You need a reconstructed body for your old redeemed soul.

When Jesus returns for the rapture, and the shout of God is made, there is going to be a reconstruction of your humanity. You and your soul will hook up again. There will be a body rising, and the dead in Christ will be resurrected with their new spiritual and glorified body. That's how you will be resurrected. He talks about people in verse 14 who fall asleep in Jesus. The assumption is that you have accepted Jesus, and if that assumption is true when you die, you fall asleep in him. He says the dead in Christ shall rise first, and then we who are alive and remain shall be caught up together with them in the clouds to meet the Lord in the air. We're not meeting him on earth because it's not time for him to come to earth yet; because we are going to move back and forth from heaven to earth. A lot of your time will be spent on earth and not in heaven.

Flesh and blood cannot inherit the kingdom of heaven. There will be a change. Paul said in 1 Corinthians 15:51 (NKJV), "Behold I tell you a mystery. We shall not all sleep, but we shall all be changed." Everybody dead or alive will go through a metamorphosis, like a butterfly emerging from a caterpillar. He says in a twinkling of an eye, at the last trumpet the dead will be raised *imperishable*, and we will be changed. The *perishable* (some Bible verses say *corruptible*) will put on *imperishable* (some Bible verses say *incorruptible*), and the mortal will put on immortality. Everything that is wrong with you will change. It will be a glorified body. What will that body be like? When we see him (at the rapture) we will be like him. If I am going to be like him, I need to know what he is like, so I'll know what I would be like when I am like him.

The apostle John said in 1 John 3:2 (NKJV), "Beloved now we are children of God, and it has not yet been revealed what we shall be; but we know that when he is revealed, we shall be like him, for we shall see him as he is."

Let's rehearse Jesus's resurrection. Three days after the crucifixion he was raised from the dead with a glorified body. When he stepped out the grave, he was the same person who died. He wasn't another person. Jesus is coming back again, so you won't become somebody other than who you are. It's not like you are metamorphosing into something else because remember—it's your soul that is entering into the body. Whatever you are is what you will be then.

The rapture is the next event on the calendar. Before God reenters Israel he's going to remove us before the wrath in order to recall his people. Paul ends by saying, "Therefore comfort one another with these words" (1 Thessalonians 4:18 NKJV). Why should this matter? You should feel a little better because to be absent from the body is to be present with the Lord. It should make you feel a little better about the uncertainty and the fear that comes with death. It should make you want to witness, so that you don't have loved ones who are left behind. It should make you want to share the gospel to make sure that on that great day, your family and friends that you love and care about are seized in the rapture with you, and not left for the hell that's going to break loose on earth in the tribulation period.

It says in 1 John 3:3 (NKJV), "And everyone who has this hope in him purifies himself, just as he is pure." Hearing this good news should affect how we live. The point is you don't want to be left behind. If you don't know for certain that your sins have been forgiven and that you have received the gift of eternal life, you have two things that can happen. You could die, or the rapture could occur.[7]

---

[7] Dr. Tony Evans, Sermon. The Rapture and the Church.

Will We Recognize Our Loved Ones?

The scripture teaches us that we will have a glorified body like his (Jesus). It says in Philippians 3:21 (NKJV), "Who will transform our lowly body that it may be conformed to his glorious body, according to the working by which he is able even to subdue all things to himself."

Matthew Henry's commentary says this about the glory reserved for the bodies: There is a glory reserved for the bodies of the saints, which they will be instated in at the resurrection. The body is now at the best a vile body—*the body of humiliation*: It has its rise and origin from the earth; it is supported out of the earth and is subject to many diseases and to death at last. It is often the occasion and instrument of many sins, which is called the *body of this death* (Romans 7:24). Or it may be understood of its vileness when it lies in the grave; at the resurrection, it will be found a vile body, resolved into rottenness and dust; *the dust will return to the earth as it was* (Ecclesiastes 12:7). But it will be made a glorious body, and not only raised again to life but also raised to great advantage. The sample of this change, and that is the glorious body of Christ when he was transfigured upon the mount, *his face did shine as the sun, and his raiment was white as the light* (Matthew 17:2). He went to heaven clothed with a body that he might take possession of the inheritance in our nature and be not only the *firstborn from the dead* but also the *firstborn of the children of the resurrection*. We shall be conformed to *the image of his Son* that he may be the *firstborn among many brethren* (Romans 8:29).[8]

In 1 Corinthians 15:35–40, 42–44 (NIV), the apostle Paul uses the seed analogy to teach us that our earthly, weak, and mortal physical bodies must die and be sown in the grave before it can be changed. The scripture says, "But someone will ask, 'How are the dead raised? With what kind of body will they come?' How foolish! What you sow does not come to life unless it dies. When you sow, you do not plant the body that will be, but just a seed, perhaps of wheat or of something else. But God gives it a body as he has determined, and to each kind of seed he gives its own body. All flesh is not the same. Men have one kind of flesh, animals have another, birds another, and fish another. There are also heavenly bodies, and there are earthly bodies; but the splendor of the heavenly bodies is one kind, and the splendor of the earthly bodies is another. So will it be with the resurrection of the dead. The body that is sown is perishable, it is raised in imperishable. It is sown in dishonor, it is raised in glory. It is sown in weakness, it is raised in power. It is sown a natural body, it is raised a spiritual body. If there is a natural body, and there is also a spiritual body."

---

[8] Matthew Henry's *Commentary on the Whole Bible*. New Modern Edition, complete and unabridged in six volumes. Ninth Edition (2009). Peabody, Massachusetts. Hendrickson Publishers Inc. (1991). *Acts to Revelation*, volume 6 of 6 volumes, pp. 598. There is a glory reserved for the bodies of the saints, which they will be instated at the resurrection.

JESUS SAID IT'S DONE (WHEN YOUR TIME IS UP)

There are many people who believe that upon their death, that they will be taken to heaven—not only to be with Jesus, but to also be with their loved ones and friends. After Jesus was resurrected from the grave, he first appeared to Mary Magdalene, and then to the disciples. He appeared to Thomas at another time because he wasn't there when he first appeared to the other disciples. They all recognized Jesus (Matthew 28:1–8 NIV, Mark 16:9, 14 NIV, Luke 24:36–41 NIV, John 20:16, 19, 24, 29–30 NIV).

When Jesus was transfigured on the Mount of Transfiguration, the three disciples that were there were able to recognize Elijah and Moses (Matthew 17:2–3 NIV, Mark 9:2–4 NIV, Luke 9:28–32 NIV). We are not told how, but the fact they were identified suggest that we will be able to recognize our loved ones and others.

According to Revelation 21, it mentions heaven when God's plan for humanity has been completed. He will create a new heaven and a new earth. He will create a new Jerusalem for our loved ones and us. The apostle John said he saw the holy city, the new Jerusalem (where those who are converted, which prayerfully will include all our loved ones) coming down from God out of heaven. Behold, the tabernacle of God is with men, and he shall dwell with them. The new heaven and new earth is discussed in another section of the book.

Based on God's word, we will recognize our loved ones and the saints of all ages. But if you are unsaved, you will not get to see your loved ones and friends. Do you want to see your loved ones again?

The Mansion

According to Titus 1:2 (NKJV), "God cannot lie," and we are told in Isaiah 55:11 (NKJV), "So shall My word be that goes forth from My mouth. It shall not return to me void. But it shall accomplish what I please. And it shall prosper in the thing which I sent it." Jesus is doing just what he said he was going to do—prepare a place for you. The Bible tells us that Jesus is coming back in due time to time to retrieve all his faithful followers to himself. *All true believers will experience happiness and peace, and they will be welcomed into their new home.* Jesus says in John 14:2 (NKJV), "In my Father's house are many mansions; if it were not so, I would have told you. I go to prepare a place for you." Prepare means to make preparation for something, not to construct something. In this house are many mansions—distinct dwellings for each believer who will spend eternity with him. He wants to give us something that is tangible to look forward to, a place where we will go to be with him. Jesus isn't preparing an apartment, a tabernacle, a condo, a town house, a single-family home, a trailer, a cottage, or a tent. This is not just any kind of mansion. This heavenly house is not made with hands, and it sits eternally in the heavens. It says in 2 Corinthians 5:1 (NIV), "Now we know that if the earthly tent we live in is destroyed, we have a building from God, an eternal house in heaven, not built by human hands." It is the Father's house, and Jesus is the King of kings and Lord of lords who reigns and rules in this house.

What makes our eternal home in heaven so unique and special? It is designed by the Master Architect, the only One who knows how to design a perfect house. Before settling into my new house, the builder's foremen took me on a walk-through. During the walk-through, I got to see the model, the layout, and all the additional amenities that I had selected and so forth. Everything appeared to look good. After settling into the house, I began to notice the flaws and imperfections. I was not pleased with the workmanship, and I regret the choices I made in selecting this builder. The flaws, imperfections, and regrets will never happen to those who have an eternal home in heaven. The eternal home has been planned and prepared by God—himself. Hebrews 11 describes how Abraham was looking forward to his eternal home. It says in Hebrews 11:10 (NKJV), "For he waited for the city which has foundations, whose builder and maker is God." The book of Revelation chapter 21 describes the ultimate care and detail that God, as the architect, has put into the plans for our eternal home.

Jesus doesn't want to leave his followers and believers with those who are miserable and are living in darkness—the ones who don't believe in him. For them, the Scripture says in 1 Corinthians 2:9 (NKJV), "Eye has not seen, nor ear heard, nor have entered into the heart of man the things which God has prepared for those who love him." Jesus says in John 14:1 (NKJV), "You believe in God, believe also in Me." Only the believers are entitled to dwell in this house.

Jesus is our sin bearer and Savior, the Lord of our life, and the One who intercedes on our behalf. He is also preparing that perfect place in heaven for those who, by his grace, have faith in him alone. This eternal house, which is perfectly designed and built, is also protected with an eternal guarantee. This will be a heavenly, magnificent, glorious, eternal home. This is a place of permanent abode—a stable dwelling. We are to rejoice in what Jesus is doing for us on earth and also for what he is doing for us in heaven. Amen and amen.

In this heavenly and holy house, we will be in our new glorified body. The old perishable (sinful) body will become imperishable (without sin), and mortality (death) will become immortality (unending existence). The old sinful nature will be gone, and all things are made new. The worldly things such as the lust of the eyes, the lust of the flesh, and the pride of life are things of the past. There will be no drinking, drugging, or smoking; no fussing or cussing; no fornication; no sickness, sorrow, pain and suffering; no trials and tribulations; no tears and heartaches; no wars; no pollution; no crimes or violence; no racism (or any other isms); no bars or clubs, no politics; no corruption; no fear, no sexual, verbal, or physical abuse, and you won't be *dropping it like it's hot, or backing that thang up*. There will be no need for automobiles, buses, trains, planes, or public transportation.

When you move into this mansion, you don't have to worry about paying mortgage, rent, late fees, property taxes, or homeowner's insurance. You don't have to worry about being evicted, or going into foreclosure. You don't have to worry about paying any bills. You don't have to worry about a heating and cooling system. You don't have to worry about replacing a light bulb, putting batteries in the smoke detector, or changing the filter in the furnace. You don't have to worry about the roof leaking, or sink or toilet stopping up. You don't have to worry about a power outage. You won't need an alarm system. You don't have to worry about this mansion being destroyed by any natural disasters, or falling into a sinkhole. This mansion will have everything that you need and more. This mansion is being prepared just for you.

The Book of Life and the Judgment Seat of Christ

There are many mansions because there will be many believers who will be brought to dwell eternally with Christ, and he knows the exact number. How does he know the exact number? Before we can enter into this beautiful mansion, Jesus wants to open up the book on your life (known as the Book of Life). *The Unger's Bible Dictionary* says this about the Book of Life:

> The Book of Life is a figurative expression originating from the ancient custom of keeping genealogical records (Nehemiah 7:5, 64; 12:22–23) and of registering citizens for numerous purposes (Jeremiah 22:30; Ezekiel 13:9). God is accordingly represented as having a record of all His creation, particularly those under His special care. To be expunged from "the book of life" is to be severed from the divine favor and to incur an untimely death. In the New Testament "the book of life" refers to the roster of righteous who are to inherit eternal life (Philippians 4:3;

Revelation 3:5; 13:8; 17:8; 21:27), from which the saved are not to be blotted out (3:5). In the Apocalypse, "the book" (or books) is presented as the divine record of the works of the unsaved at the great white throne of judgment (Revelation 20:12, 15), according to which the lost will suffer degrees of eternal punishment.[9]

Matthew Henry's commentary says this about the Book of life:

> A great reward promised to the conquering Christian, and it is very much the same with what has been already mentioned: He that *overcometh shall be clothed in white raiment.* The purity of grace shall be rewarded with the perfect purity of glory. Holiness, when perfected shall be its own reward; glory is the perfection of grace, differing not in kind, but in degree. Now to this added another promise very suitable to the case: *I will not blot his name out of the book of life, but will confess his name before my Father, and before his angels.* Christ has his book of life, a register and roll of all who shall inherit eter-

---

[9] Merrill F. Unger. *Unger's Bible Dictionary*, revised and updated edition (1988). The Moody Bible Institute of Chicago, pp. 178. The Book of Life refers to the roster of righteous who are to inherit eternal life, from which the saved are not blotted out.

nal life. The book of eternal election: The book of remembrance of all those who have lived to God, and have kept up the life and power of godliness in evil times. Christ will not blot the names of his chosen and faithful ones out of this book of life. Men may be enrolled in the registers of the church as baptized, as making a profession, as having a name to live, and that name may come to be blotted out of the roll when it appears that it was but a name. A name to live without spiritual life often lose the very name before they die, and they are left of God to blot out their own names by their gross and open wickedness. But the names of those that overcome shall never be blotted out. Christ will produce this book of life, and confess the names of the faithful who stand there before God and all the angels. He will do this as their Judge when the books shall be opened. He will do this as their captain and head leading them with him triumphantly to heaven, and presenting them to the Father: *Behold me, and the children that thou has given me.* How great will this honor and reward be![10]

---

[10] Matthew Henry's *Commentary on the Whole Bible*, New Modern Edition, complete and unabridged in six volumes. Ninth Edition (2009). Peabody, Massachusetts. Hendrickson Publishers Inc. (1991). *Acts to Revelation*, volume

It says in Exodus 32:33 (NKJV), "Whoever has sinned against Me, I will blot him out of My book." Is your name written in the book, or will it be blotted out?

According to the *New Strong's Exhaustive Concordance of the Bible*, the Greek word for judgment seat is *bēma* (a step). *Unger's Bible Dictionary* defines it as a raised place mounted by steps used by the official seat of a judge, and he says this about the judgment seat of Christ:

> This judgment is spoken of in 2 Corinthians 5:10, "For we must all appear before the judgment seat of Christ, that each one may be recompensed for his deeds in the body, according to what he has done, whether good or bad." The manifestation of the believer's works is in question in this judgment. It is most emphatically not a judgment of the believer's sins. These have been fully atoned for in the vicarious and substitutionary death of Christ, and remembered no more (Hebrews 10:17). It is quite necessary, however, that the service of every child of God be definitely scrutinized and evaluated (Matthew 12:36; Romans 14:10; Galatians 6:7; Ephesians 6:8; Colossians 3:24–25). As a result of this judgment of the believer's works, there will be reward or loss of reward. In any event, the truly born-again believer will be saved (1 Corinthians 3:11–15). The judgment seat, literally *bēma*, evidently is set up in heaven previous to Christ's glorious second advent to establish his earth rule in the millennial kingdom (Matthew 16:27; 2 Timothy 4:8; Revelation 22:12). The out-taking of the church, accord-

---

6 of 6 volumes, pp. 912. I will not blot his name out of the Book of Life, but will confess his name before my Father and before angels.

ing to 1 Thessalonians 4:13–18; 1 Corinthians 15:51–58, must first be fulfilled. The judgment seat of Christ is necessary for the appointment of places of rulership and authority within his role of "King of kings and Lord of lords" at his revelation in power to glory.[11]

All humanity will be judged. It says in Romans 14:10 (NKJV), "For we shall all stand before the judgment seat of Christ." The scenario will be like going to court (you are on trial), but you are without representation. You will not have legal counsel or an attorney, and there will be no family members or others there to support you. You will be on your own, standing before Jesus who will be the judge. You can't change or deny what's already written in the "book" about your life. The evidence of how you treat one another and how you spend your time, talents, and treasures on earth will be all the proof that the Judge needs. All humanity will be held accountable for the deeds committed in their life while on earth (Romans 14:12 NKJV), and everyone will be judged fairly. God is a just God, and he is a righteous God. The scripture says:

> And as it is appointed for men to die once; but after this judgment. (Hebrews 9:27 NKJV)

The following will be judged: the unsaved, the dead of all time, the devil, the fallen angels, the believers, and all

---

[11] Merrill F. Unger. *Unger's Bible Dictionary*, revised and updated edition (1988). The Moody Bible Institute of Chicago, pp. 728. All must appear before the judgment seat of Christ that each one may be recompensed for his deed in the body according to what he has done.

the wicked who ever lived. The one who believes in Christ has been released from judgment. Jesus says in John 5:24 (NKJV), "Most assuredly, I say to you, he who hears my word and believes in him who sent me has everlasting life, and shall not come into judgment, but has passed from death into life," and in Romans 8:1 (NKJV), "There is therefore now no condemnation to those who are in Christ Jesus, who do not walk according to the flesh, but according to the Spirit." The Bible speaks of the white throne of judgment, and according to *Unger's Bible Dictionary*, the following is stated:

> This last great judgment comprehends the judgment of all unsaved of all ages (Revelation 20:11–5). The basis will be works, which evidently suggests differences and degrees of punishment. All who are not found in "the book of life" are cast into "the lake of fire." This is called "the second death," which means final and complete cutting off from God's presence and a sin-cleansed universe.[12]

Additional reading scriptures about judgment are found in Psalm 9:7–8, 96:13, 98:9; Ecclesiastes 11:9, 12:14 (NKJV), 1 Corinthians 6:3 (NKJV); 2 Peter 2:4 (NKJV); Jude 6, 15 (NKJV); and Revelation 11:18, 20:12–13 (NKJV).

---

[12] Ibid., pp. 727. The last great judgment is called the white throne of judgment. All who are not found in the Book of Life are cast into the lake of fire.

When your life is over on earth, and when it comes time for you to stand before Jesus, will he say, "Well done, good and faithful servant, you were faithful over a few things, I will make you ruler over many things. Enter into the joy of your Lord" (Matthew 25:21 NKJV), or will he say, "I tell you I do not know you, where are you from. Depart from me, all you workers of iniquity" (Luke 13:27 NKJV; Matthew 7:23, 25:41 NKJV).

Heaven and Hell

Randy Alcorn is the founder of External Ministries, a non-profit ministry dedicated to teaching the principles of God's word and assisting the church in ministering to the unreached, unfed, unborn, uneducated, unreconciled, and unsupported people around the world. He served as a pastor and holds a degree in theology and biblical studies, and has taught at various universities and seminaries. He is the author of more than forty books. According to his book titled *Heaven*, the author shares with us the writings of others on how some civilizations down through the years view the afterlife.

The sense that we will live forever somewhere has shaped every civilization in human history. Australian aborigines pictured heaven as a distant island beyond the western horizon. The early Finns thought it was an island in the faraway east. Mexicans, Peruvians, and Polynesians believed that they went to the sun or moon after death.[13] Native Americans believed that in the afterlife, their spirits would hunt the spirits of buffalo. The Gilgamesh epic and ancient Babylonian legend refers to a resting place of heroes and hints at a tree of life.[14] In the pyramids of Egypt, the

---

[13] J. Sidlow Baxter. Native Americans believed that in the afterlife their spirits would hunt the spirits of buffalo.

[14] Harvey Minkoff. In the pyramids of Egypt, the embalmed bodies had maps placed beside them as a guide to the future world.

embalmed bodies had maps placed beside them as guides to the future world.[15] The Romans believed that the righteous would picnic in the Elysian Fields while their horses grazed nearby. Although these depictions of the afterlife differ, the unifying testimony of the human heart throughout history is belief in the after death. Anthropological evidence suggests that every culture has a God-given innate sense of the eternal, and that this world is not all there is.[16]

Heaven and hell are real, and the Bible talks about both. Heaven is the highest and holiest place. Heaven is where Jesus resides. He sits at the right hand of his Father, and that's where we should desire to be with him. It says in Colossians 3:1–4 (NKJV), "If then you were raised with Christ, seek those things which are above, where Christ is sitting at the right hand of God. Set your mind on things above, not on things on the earth. For you died, and your life is hidden with Christ in God. When Christ who is our life appears, then you also will appear with him in glory." As Christians, we should know that this world is not our home; we are only passing by. It says in Philippians 3:20 (NKJV), "For our citizenship is in heaven, from which we also eagerly wait for the Savior, the Lord Jesus Christ." Matthew Henry's commentary says this about heaven:

> This world is not our home, but there our greatest privileges and concerns lie. And because our citizenship is there, our

---

[15] Edward Donnelly. The Romans believed that the righteous would picnic in the Elysian fields while their horses grazed nearby.

[16] Don Richardson. Anthropological evidence suggests that every culture has a God-given innate sense of the eternal – that this world is not all there is.

conversation is there; and being related to that world we keep up a correspondence with it. The life of a Christian is in heaven where his head is, and his home is, and where he hopes to be shortly. He sets his affections upon things above, and where his heart is there will his conversation be.[17] We must store these things up in our hearts. The scripture says in Matthew 6:21 (NKJV), "For where your treasure is, there your heart will be also."

It says in John 3:13 (NKJV), "No one has ascended to heaven but he who came down from heaven, that is, the Son of Man who is in heaven." Merrill F. Unger was an American Bible commentator, scholar, archaeologist, and theologian. He authored many books, such as the *Unger's Bible Dictionary*, and he shares with us the following about the ascension of Jesus Christ. The ascension of Christ is his glorious withdrawal of his bodily presence from the earth, and his entrance as the God-man and mediatorial King into heaven. These are the facts about the ascension. The ascension took place from the Mount of Olives forty days after the resurrection. This was predicted in Psalm 68:18, 110:1 (NKJV), interpreted in Ephesians 4:8–10 (NKJV), Hebrews 1:13, and by Jesus himself in John 6:62,

---

[17] Matthew Henry's *Commentary on the Whole Bible*. New Modern Edition, complete and unabridged in six volumes. Ninth Edition (2009). Peabody, Massachusetts. Hendrickson Publishers Inc. (1991), *Acts to Revelation*, volume 6 of 6 volumes, pp. 598. This world is not our home. The believer's citizenship is in heaven and their conversations should be focused on things that are above.

20:17 (NKJV). It is recorded in Mark 16:19 (NKJV), Luke 24:50–51 (NKJV), and Acts 1:9–11 (NKJV). It was recognized by the apostle John and others (2 Corinthians 13:4 NKJV; Ephesians 2:6, 4:8–10 NKJV; 1 Peter 3:22 NKJV; 1 Timothy 3:16 NKJV; Hebrews 1:13 NKJV). It was certified by the disciples who were eyewitnesses, by the words of the two angels, by Stephen, Paul, and John who saw Christ in his ascended state (Acts 1:9–11, 7:55–56, 9:3–5 NKJV; Revelation 1:9–18 NKJV). It was demonstrated by the descent of the Holy Spirit on the Day of Pentecost (Matthew 3:11 NKJV; Luke 24:49 NKJV; Acts 2:1–4, 33 NKJV), and by the manifold gifts bestowed by the ascended Lord upon his church (Ephesians 4:11–12 NKJV).

These are the doctrinal and ethical significance of the ascension. The visible ascension of Christ was necessary and a seal of his resurrection (Romans 6:9 NKJV). It was the connecting link between his humiliation and glorification (Philippians 2:5–11 NKJV). It was the removal of his bodily, but not his spiritual presence from the earth. Christ has passed the heavens, but invisibly he is always near at hand (Hebrews 4:14 NKJV, Matthew 28:20 NKJV, Acts 23:11 NKJV, 2 Timothy 4:17 NKJV). He has the power and dominion in heaven and earth. He sits at the right hand of the Father on the throne of God (Matthew 28:18 NKJV, Philippians 2:10 NKJV, Hebrews 12:2 NKJV). He is the perpetual intercession of Christ as our great High Priest (Romans 8:34 NKJV, Hebrews 5:10, 7:25 NKJV). He sent forth the Holy Spirit and bestowed other gifts upon the church (Acts 2:33 NKJV, Ephesians 4:11–12 NKJV). He is their heavenly advocate (1 John 2:1 NKJV). He is interceding for their perfection (John 17:20–24 NKJV). The believer is encouraged to fidelity and to prayer (Hebrews 4:14–16 NKJV). He awaits his perfected triumph over all his foes (Hebrews 10:13 NKJV). He will come again to judge the world (Matthew 25:31–32 NKJV, Acts 1:11 NKJV).[18]

Mr. Unger shares with us the writings of others on the subject of heaven:

> Scripture evidently specifies three heavens, since "the third heaven" is revealed to exist (2 Corinthians 12:2), and it is logical that a third heaven cannot exist without a first and second. Scripture does not describe specifically the first and second heaven. The first, however, apparently refers to the atmospheric heavens of the birds (Hosea 2:18 "sky") and of clouds (Daniel 7:13). The second heaven may be the stellar spaces (cf. Genesis 1:14–18). It is the abode of all supernatural angelic beings. The third heaven is the abode of the Triune God. Its location is unrevealed. It is the divine plan at pres-

---

[18] Merrill F. Unger's bibliography references: H. B. Swete, *The Ascended Christ* (1911); C. F. D. Moule, *Expository Times* 68 (1957); 205–9; W. J. Sparrow-Simpson, *Our Lord's Resurrection* (1964); id., *The Resurrection and the Christian* (1968); W. Milligan, *The Ascension of Christ* (1980); P. Toon, *The Ascension of Our Lord* (1984). The ascension of Jesus Christ and the doctrinal and ethical significance.

ent to populate the third heaven. It is a place (John 14:1–3). It is called "glory" (Hebrews 2:10); those who enter it will be perfected forever (10:14) and made partakers of Christ's fullness (John 1:16), which is all fullness (Colossians 1:19), and which comprehends the very nature of the Godhead bodily (2:9). Heaven is a place of beauty (Revelation 21:1, 22:7) of life (1 Timothy 4:8), service (Revelation 22:3), worship (Revelation 19:1–3), and glory (2 Corinthians 4:17–18).[19]

Visions and revelations were given to Isaiah, Ezekiel, Paul, and John about God, the new heaven, and the new earth. The scriptures below explain what they saw.

It says in Isaiah 65:17–23, 66:22 (NKJV),

> For behold, I create new heavens and a new earth. And the former shall not be remembered or come to mind. But be glad and rejoice forever in what I create. For behold, I create Jerusalem as a rejoicing, and her people a joy. I will rejoice in Jerusalem, and joy in my people. The voice of weeping shall no longer be heard in her; nor the voice of crying. No more

---

[19] Ibid. Bibliography references: E. M. Bounds. *Heaven: A Place, a City, a Home* (1921); W. M. Smith. *The Biblical Doctrine of Heaven* (1968); N. Turner. *Christian Words* (1982), pp. 202–05. *Heaven*, the abode of the Triune God, a place of beauty, life, service, worship, and glory.

shall an infant from there live but a few days, nor an old man who has not fulfilled his days. For the child shall die one hundred years old. But the sinner being one hundred years old shall be accursed. They shall build houses and inhabit them. They shall plant vineyards and eat their fruit. They shall not build and another inhabit. They will not plant and another eat. For as the days of a tree, so shall be the days of my people. And my elect shall long enjoy the work of their hands. They shall not labor in vain. Nor bring forth children for trouble. They shall be the descendants of the blessed of the LORD, and their offspring with them. For as the new heavens and the new earth which I will make shall remain before me, says the LORD. So shall your descendants and your name remain.

It says in Ezekiel 1:26–28 (NKJV),

And above the firmament over their heads was the likeness of a throne, in appearance like a sapphire stone; on the likeness of the throne was a likeness with the appearance of a man high above it. Also from the appearance of his waist and upward I saw, as it were, the color of amber with the appearance of fire all around within it; and from the appearance of his waist and downward I saw, as it were, the appearance of fire with brightness all around. Like the appearance of a rainbow in a cloud on a rainy day, so was the appearance of the brightness all around it. This was the appearance of the likeness of the glory of the Lord. So when I saw it, I fell on my face, and I heard a voice of one speaking.

Paul says in 2 Corinthians 12:1–4, 7 (NKJV),

> It is doubtless not profitable for me to boast. I will come to visions and revelations of the Lord. I know a man in Christ who fourteen years ago, whether in the body I do not know, or whether out of the body I do not know. God knows such a one was caught up to the third heaven. And I know such a man, whether in the body, or out of the body I do not know. God knows. How he was caught up into Paradise, and heard inexpressible words, which it is not lawful for a man to utter. And lest I should be exalted above measure by the abundance of the revelations, a thorn in the flesh was given to me, a messenger of Satan to buffet me, lest I be exalted above measure.

The last book of the Bible is Revelation. It's identified as the revelation of Jesus Christ. The word *revelation* means unveiling. It's the unveiling of Jesus future plan for the earth, and for his redeemed saints both for time and eternity. In chapter 21, is the unveiling of the new heaven and new earth.

John says in Revelation 21:1–5, 10 (NKJV),

> Now I saw a new heaven and a new earth, for the first heaven and the first earth had passed away. Also, there was no more sea. Then I, John, saw the holy city, a new Jerusalem coming down out of heaven from God, prepared as a bride adorned for her husband. And I heard a loud voice from heaven saying, behold, the tabernacle of God is with men, and he will dwell with them, and they shall be his people. God himself will be with them and be their God. And God will wipe away every tear from their eyes; there shall be no more death, nor sorrow, no crying. There shall be no more pain, for the former things have passed away. Then he who sat on the throne said, behold, I make all things new. And he said to me, write, for these words are true and faithful. He carried him away in the Spirit to a great and high mountain, and showed me the great

city, the holy Jerusalem descending out of heaven from God.

John goes into further detail in Revelation chapter 21. He was being carried away in the Spirit to a high mountain. There, God showed him the Holy City, Jerusalem, coming down out of heaven. He saw the glory of God, all its beauty and brilliance, and seeing it was like looking at precious jewels. The wall was high with twelve gates, and there were twelve angels at the gates. The names of the twelve tribes of Israel were written on the gates, and the gates covered the four corners of the world (east, north, south, and west). The wall of the city had twelve foundations, and written on them were the names of the twelve apostles (Jesus disciples). He tells us what was used to measure the gates and walls and the length, breadth, and height? He identified the precious stones used to construct the walls, gates, and foundation. The street would be paved with gold. There would be no need for the sun or moon to shine because the glory of the Lamb (Jesus) would illuminate the city. All those who are saved will walk in this marvelous light and bring their glory and honor to it. The gates won't be closed by day, and there will be no night. Nothing that's an abomination to God can enter into the gates. Only those who are written in the Lamb's Book of Life will enter into the new Jerusalem. The New Jerusalem is described as a paradise. The former paradise was lost by sin of the first Adam, and this new paradise is restored by the second Adam (Jesus). Only two people occupied this first paradise (Adam and

Eve), but in the second paradise, cities and nations will be the occupants.

In the next chapter (22), the angel of the Lord showed John the "pure river of water of life." Matthew Henry describes the "pure river of water," and the "fruitful tree of life." The river that is mentioned is described by its fountainhead, which is the throne of God and the Lamb (Jesus). It says in Revelation 21:6 (NKJV), "I will give of the fountain of the water of life freely to them who thirsts." From this water flows the springs of grace, comfort, and glory, which are all in God, and it will flow to you. This river is described as clear and crystal. There are no pollutants in the water. In contrast to the streams of earthly comfort, they were dirty and muddy, but these streams that the Lamb gives is clear and refreshing which will give and preserve the life of those who drink of them.

The tree of life is in this paradise. There was such a tree in the earthly paradise. It says in Genesis 2:9 (NKJV), "And out of the ground the Lord God made every tree grow that is pleasant to the sight and good for food. The tree of life was also in the midst of the garden, and the tree of knowledge of good and evil." This new tree of life excels the previous one. This tree is fed by the pure waters of the river, and it will flow from the throne of God. The glory and blessedness of God will supply all the glory and blessedness of heaven.

The fruitfulness of the tree will produce all kinds of fruit, and it will be pleasant and wholesome for the saints. This tree will never be empty or barren; there will always be fruit. There will be a continuance of the fruit, and it will always be fresh. The presence of God in heaven is the well-being and happiness of the saints. In him they will find a remedy for all former maladies and are preserved by him in the most vigorous state.

There will be freedom from evil. There will be no more curse or accursed one and no serpent, as it was in the earthly paradise. The devil has nothing to do, and he cannot prevent the saints from serving and being subjective to God, as he did to Adam and Eve.

The supreme happiness of the state of the saints is seeing the face of God, and to behold his beauty. God will have ownership over them, and he will place a seal and name on their foreheads. The saints will reign with him forever.[20]

Verses 6–19 speak of the following. Jesus sent his angels to John to show him the things that were deemed faithful and true, the things that must be done, and to reveal them to the world. These things must be done, because Jesus said, "he will come quickly." And he will do away with the doubters and prove those who have believed and kept his words. The reason the book of prophecy was to be left opened is to be examined and studied by all in hopes that they might understand it. God did not speak in secret; he deals freely and openly with all, but calls everyone to witness the declarations that are made.

Because the time is drawing near, God said in verse 11, "He who is unjust, let him be unjust still. He who is

---

[20] Matthew Henry's *Commentary on the Whole Bible*. New Modern Edition, complete and unabridged in six volumes. Ninth Edition (2009). Peabody, Massachusetts. Hendrickson Publishers Inc (1991). *Acts to Revelation*, volume 6 of 6 volumes, pp. 954-955. The pure river of water, and the fruitful tree of life.

filthy, let him be filthy still. He who is righteous, let him be righteous still. He who is holy, let him be holy still." He says again, "Behold, I am coming quickly." And he said this several times: "I am the Alpha and Omega, the beginning and the end."

He says in his word that those who do his commandments are blessed, they will have the right to the tree of life, and they can enter into the gates into the city. The ones on the outside (evil and wicked) cannot enter into the gates. The Spirit and the bride says, "Come and let him who thirst come. Whoever desires, let him take the water of life freely."

When Lucifer was in heaven, he was one of God's highest angels. His glorious unfallen state is described in Ezekiel 28:12–15 (NKJV),

> You were the seal of perfection. You were full of wisdom and perfect in beauty. You were in Eden, the garden of God. Every precious stone was your covering: the sardius, topaz, diamond, beryl, onyx, jasper, sapphire, turquoise, and emerald with gold. The workmanship of your timbrels and pipes was prepared for you on the day you were created. You were the anointed cherub (angel) who covers. I established you. You were on the holy mountain of God. You walked back and forth in the midst of fiery stones. You were perfect in

your ways from the day you were created, until iniquity was found in you.

Lucifer was kicked right out of heaven. The fall of Lucifer is explained in Isaiah 14:12–15 (NKJV),

> How you are fallen from heaven. O Lucifer, son of the morning. How you are cut down to the ground, you who weakened the nations. For you said in your heart I will ascend into heaven. I will exalt my throne above the stars of God. I will also sit on the mount of the congregation on the farthest sides of the north. I will ascend above the heights of the clouds. I will be like the Most High. Yet you shall be brought down to Sheol, to the lowest depths of the pit.

There was a war between God's angels and with the dragon and his angels as explained in Revelation 12:7–10 (NKJV):

> And war broke out in heaven. Michael (God's angel) and his angels fought with the dragon; and the dragon and his angels fought. But they did not prevail, nor was a place found for them in heaven any longer. So the great dragon was cast out, that serpent of old, called the Devil and

> Satan, who deceives the whole world; he was cast to the earth, and his angels with him. Then I heard a loud voice saying in heaven: "Now salvation and strength, and the kingdom of our God, and the power of his Christ have come for the accuser of our brethren; who accused them before our God day and night has been cast down."

He became rebellious and prideful. Look at how many times he exalts himself and says "I" in Isaiah 14:12–15. He wanted to make it all about himself. He wanted to be like God. He wanted to be in charge and take God's place. But God was the one who created him. It says in his word: Do not let the rebellious exalt themselves (Psalm 66:7), and Proverbs 16:18–19 (NKJV),

> Pride goes before destruction; and a haughty spirit before a fall. Better to be of a humble spirit with the lowly than to divide the spoil with the proud.

Since he was booted out heaven, he is no longer known as Lucifer. He has many names, but now he is known as Satan or the devil. Some people laugh at the idea of a devil. They see him as some sort of cartoon character in long red underwear with horns and a tail, holding a pitch fork. The devil is a present-day reality. Jesus says in John 10:10 (NKJV), "The thief (devil) does not come except to steal, kill, and destroy. I have come that they may have life, and that they may have it more abundantly." He is the enemy, and he will use anybody and anything to give you a distorted view of God's word, his people, and heaven. He is a liar, blasphemer, and hater.

Jesus says in John 8:44 (NKJV), "You are of your father the devil, and the desires of your father you want to do. He was a murderer from the beginning, and does not stand in the truth, because there is no truth in him. When he speaks a lie, he speaks from his own resources, for he is a liar and the father of it." He is a blasphemer, and it says in Revelation 13:6 (NKJV), "Then he opened his mouth in blasphemy against God, to blaspheme his name, his tabernacle, and those who dwell in heaven."

He hates God's people. He hates us because we are entitled to the home he was evicted out of. He is no longer welcomed, and there is nothing he can do to gain access. He doesn't want us to be in heaven with Jesus. He wants to get us in a mind game of looking at what's happening in this fallen world, instead of focusing on where Jesus is—in heaven. If we buy into this mental game at looking at the world, we will never get to experience the future plans that God has for us, which is spending eternity with Jesus and to bathe in the beauty of his fullness and glory.

Hell is the lowest place, and sometimes it's referred to as the abyss or a pit. Hell and Hades occur in the King James Version (KJV) of the Bible. Hades occurs several times in the original, in the National American Standard Bible (NASB), and in the New International Version (NIV). Some Bibles refer to hell or Hades as a grave. You can read about hell and Hades in the following scriptures: Matthew 11:23, 16:18; Luke 10:15, 16:23; Acts 2:27, 31; Revelation 1:18, 6:8, 20:13–14.

Hell will be a place for future punishment for the evil, wicked, and those who have done horrible deeds while on earth. It says in Revelation 21:8 (NKJV),

> But the cowardly, unbelieving, abominable, murderers, sexually immoral, sorcerers, idolaters, and all liars shall have their part in the lake which burns with fire and brimstone, which is the second death.

Hell will be a place of uncontrollable weeping and gnashing of teeth, misery, suffering, and everlasting torment. (See Matthew 8:12, 13:42, 13:50, 22:13, 24:51, 25:30 NKJV; Luke 13:28 NKJV.) The wicked and those who have forgotten about Jesus will end up in hell. It says in Psalm 9:17 (NKJV), "The wicked shall be turned into hell and all the nations that forgot God." And in Matthew 25:41 (NKJV), Jesus said to them, "Then he will also say to those on the left hand, depart from me, you cursed into the everlasting fire prepared for the devil and his angels."

There will be no relief for the unsaved and the wicked. They will be confined to a place of punishment and everlasting destruction for their sins. Those who enter into hell will be in a conscious state. They will suffer severely. They will have no comfort or peace. They will not be able to escape their torment. There will be no hope for them (Luke 16:19–31 NKJV). It says in Matthew 25:46 (NKJV), "And these will go away into everlasting punishment, but the righteous into eternal life." The duration of hell will be for all eternity.

God is a consuming fire (Hebrews 12:29 NKJV). Fire is symbol of God's burning judgment. It says in Isaiah 66:15 (NKJV),

> For behold, the LORD will come with fire, and with his chariots like a whirlwind. To render his anger with fury, and his rebuke with flames of fire. For by fire and by his sword the LORD will judge all flesh. And the slain of the LORD will be many.

Those who haven't repented of their sins and accepted Jesus Christ as their Lord and Savior cannot enter the presence of a holy and righteous God. They will be confined to a place of everlasting punishment and destruction. It says in Matthew 13:40–42 (NKJV),

> Therefore as the tares are gathered and burned in the fire, so it will be at the end of this age. The Son of Man will send out his angels, and they will gather out of his kingdom all things that offend, and those who practice lawlessness. And will cast them into the furnace of fire. There will be wailing and gnashing of teeth.

JESUS SAID IT'S DONE (WHEN YOUR TIME IS UP)

Now based on what you read and learned, why would some people tell someone to go to hell? The hell that some think they are experiencing on earth will be nothing compared to the hell that Jesus has prepared for them who don't believe in him. When Jesus says depart from me, to the left, to the left—this will be your last chance to do your favorite line dance.

The Believer's Rewards

Rewards are offered by God to a believer on the basis of faithful service rendered after salvation. Mr. Unger says this about rewards:

> It is clear from Scripture that God offers to the *lost* salvation and for the faithful service of the *saved*, rewards. Salvation is a free gift (John 4:10; Romans 6:23; Ephesians 2:8–9), whereas rewards are earned by works (Matthew 10:42; cf. Luke 19:17; 1 Corinthians 9:24–25; 2 Timothy 4:7–8). Salvation is a present possession (Luke 7:50; John 5:24). On the other hand, rewards are future attainments to be dispersed at the second coming of Christ for his own (Matthew 16:27; 2 Timothy 4:8). Rewards will be dispensed at the judgment seat of Christ (2 Corinthians 5:10; Romans 14:10). The doctrine of rewards is inseparably connected with God's grace. A soul is saved on the basis of divine grace; there is no room for the building up of merit on the

part of the believer. Yet God recognizes an obligation on his part to reward his saved ones for their service to him. Nothing can be done to merit salvation, but what the believer has achieved for God's glory. God recognizes with rewards at the judgment seat of Christ.[21]

It says in Matthew 16:27 (NKJV), "For the Son of Man will come in the glory of his Father with his angels, and then he will reward each according to his works."

A crown is given as a reward of victory. It is to bestow something upon someone as a mark of honor or recompense. It says in 1 Corinthians 3:14 (NKJV), "If anyone's work which he has built on it endures, he will receive a reward." It says in Revelation 22:12 (NKJV), "And behold I am coming quickly and my reward is with me to give to everyone according to his work." There are five crowns mentioned in the New Testament of the Bible. They are the incorruptible crown, the crown of righteousness, the crown of joy, the crown of glory, and the crown of life. Each crown is described as follows, along with the scriptures.

The incorruptible crown is given to those who run life's race faithfully. It says in 1 Corinthians 9:25 (KJV), "And every man who striveth for the mastery is temperate in all things. Now they do it to obtain a corruptible crown, but we for an incorruptible." Those who conquered

---

[21] Merrill F. Unger's *Bible Dictionary*, revised and updated edition (1988). The Moody Bible Institute of Chicago, pp. 1080. God offers the believer rewards based on their faithful service rendered after salvation.

in these games were crowned only with the withering leaves or boughs of trees, of olive, bays, or laurel. But the Christians have an incorruptible crown in view, a crown of glory that never fadeth away, an inheritance incorruptible, reserved in heaven for them. And would they suffer themselves to be outdone by these racers or wrestlers? And shall not Christians, who hope for the approval of the sovereign Judge and a crown of glory from his hands, stretch forward in the heavenly race and exert themselves in beating down their fleshly inclinations and the strongholds of sin? The racers in these games run at uncertainty. All run, but one receives the prize. Every racer, therefore, is at a great uncertainty whether he shall win it or not. But the Christian racer is at no such uncertainty. Every one may run here so as to obtain, but then he must run within the lines; he must keep to the path of duty prescribed, which, some think, is the meaning of running not as uncertainty. He who keeps within the limits prescribed and keeps on in his race will never miss his crown, though others may get theirs before him.[22] The race isn't given to the swift, but to the one who endures to the end. In this life we will be tested, face trials and tribulations, and encounter pain and suffering; however, in this race, the body must be made to serve the mind, and not be lord over it.

The crown of righteousness is given to those believers who love his appearing. It says in 2 Timothy 4:8 (KJV),

---

[22] Matthew Henry's *Commentary on the Whole Bible*. New Modern Edition, complete and unabridged in six volumes. Ninth Edition (2009). Peabody, Massachusetts. Hendrickson Publishers Inc. (1991). *Acts to Revelation*, volume 6 of 6 volumes, pp. 445–446. The incorruptible crown is given to the believers who overcome and endure trials and temptations.

"Henceforth, there is laid up for me the crown of righteousness, which the Lord, the righteous judge shall give me on that day: and not to me only; but unto all of them also that love his appearing." It is called a crown of righteousness because it will be the recompense of our services, which God is not unrighteous to forget. It is the character of all the saints that they love the appearing of Jesus Christ: They loved his first appearing when he appeared to take away sin by the sacrifice of himself (Hebrews 9:26); they love to think of it; they love his second appearing at the great day—love it and long for it; and with respect to those who love the appearing of Jesus Christ, he shall appear to their joy; there is a crown of righteousness reserved for them, which shall be given to them (Hebrews 9:28). We learn: First, the Lord is the righteous Judge, for his judgment is according to the truth. Second, the crown of believers is a crown of righteousness purchased by Christ and is bestowed as the reward of the saints' righteousness. Third, this crown, which believers shall wear, is laid up for them; they have it not at present, for here they are but heirs; they have it not in possession, and yet it is sure, for it is laid up for them. Fourth, the righteous Judge will give it to all those who love, prepare, and long for his appearing.[23] It says in Revelation 22:20 (NKJV), "He who testifies to these things says, 'Surely I am coming quickly.' Amen, even so, come Lord Jesus!"

The crown of joy is given to those who show mutual love and affection towards each other and rejoice together,

---

[23] Ibid., volume 6 of 6 volumes, pp. 684. The crown of righteousness is the recompense of the believer's service, which God is not unrighteous to forget.

especially at the coming of Jesus Christ. It says in 1 Thessalonians 2:19 (KJV), "For what is our hope, or joy, or crown of rejoicing? Are not even ye in the presence of our Lord Jesus Christ at his coming?" It is a happy feeling when ministers and people have such mutual affection and esteem for one another, and especially with those who sow and those who reap shall rejoice together *in the presence of our Lord Jesus Christ at his coming*. The apostle Paul puts the Thessalonians in mind that though he could not come to them, our Lord Jesus Christ will come, and nothing shall hinder this. And further, when he shall come, all must appear in his presence, or before him, and the faithful people will be the glory and joy of faithful ministers in that great and glorious day.[24]

The crown of glory is given to faithful pastors and shepherds. It says in 1 Peter 5:2–4 (KJV),

> Feed the flock of God which is among you, taking the oversight thereof, not by constraint but willingly, not for filthy lucre but of a ready mind. Neither as being lords over God's heritage but being an example to the flock. And when the Chief Shepherd shall appear, ye shall receive a crown of glory that fadeth not away.

---

[24] Ibid., volume 6 of 6 volumes, pp. 627. The crown of joy is given to the believers who show mutual love and affection toward each other and rejoice together in the Second Coming of Jesus Christ.

Those who God has anointed, appointed, and called to preach and teach the word of God should carefully study their own duty, as well as teach the people theirs. The pastoral duty is threefold: *to feed the flock*, by preaching to them the sincere word of God and ruling them according to such directions and discipline as the word of God prescribes, both of which are implied in this expression; *feed the flock*. The pastors of the church must *take oversight thereof*. The elders are exhorted to the office of bishops (as the word signifies) by personal care and vigilance over all the flock committed to their charge. They must *be examples to the flock* and practice holiness, self-denial, mortification, and all other Christian duties, which they preach and recommend to their people. The pastors of the church ought to consider their people *as the flock of God, as God's heritage*, and treat them accordingly. They are not theirs to be lorded over at pleasure, but they are God's people and should be treated with love, meekness, and tenderness, for the sake of him to whom they belong. Those ministers who are either driven to the work by necessity or drawn to it by filthy lucre can never perform their duty as they ought because they do not do it willingly, and with a ready mind. The best way a minister can take to engage the respect of a people is to discharge his own duty among them in the best manner that he can and to be a constant example to them of all that is good. Jesus Christ is the *chief shepherd* of the whole flock and the heritage of God. He brought them and rules them; he defends and saves them forever. He is also the chief shepherd over all inferior shepherds; they derive their authority from him, act in his name, and are accountable to him at last. This chief shepherd will appear to judge all ministers and under-shepherds, to call them to account, whether they have faithfully discharged their duty both publicly and privately, according to the foregoing directions. Those who are found to have done their duty shall have what is infinitely better than temporal gain; they shall receive from the grand shepherd a high degree of everlasting glory, *a crown of glory that fadeth not away.*[25]

The crown of life is given to martyrs and those who are persecuted for their faith and endure temptation. It says in James 1:12 (KJV),

> Blessed is the man who endureth temptation: for when he is tried, he shall receive the crown of life, which the Lord has promised to those who love him.

Then the scripture says in Revelation 2:10 (KJV),

> Fear none of those things which thou shalt suffer: behold, the devil shall cast some of you into prison, that ye may be tried, and ye shall have tribulation ten days: be thou faithful unto death, and I will give thee a crown of life.

---

[25] Ibid., volume 6 of 6 volumes, pp. 832–833. The crown of glory is given to the faithful preachers and teachers who feed the flock, be an example of holiness, and carry out their duties as God prescribed.

JESUS SAID IT'S DONE (WHEN YOUR TIME IS UP)

A blessing is pronounced on those who endure their exercises and trials, as here directed: *Blessed is the man that endureth temptation.* It is not the man who suffers only that is blessed, but he who endures, who with patience and constancy goes through all difficulties in the way of his duty. Sufferings and temptations are the way to eternal blessedness: *When he is tried, he shall receive the crown of life.* To be approved by God is the great aim of a Christian in all his trials, and it will be his blessedness at last when he shall receive the crown of life. The tried Christian shall be a crowned one: and the crown he shall wear will be a crown of life. It will be life and bliss to him and will last forever. We will only bear the cross for a while, but we shall wear the crown to eternity. This blessedness involved in a crown of life is a promised thing to the righteous sufferer. The crown of life is promised not only to great and eminent saints; but also to all those who have the love of God reigning in their hearts. Every soul that truly loves God shall have its trials in this world recompensed in that world above *where love is made perfect.*[26]

It says in Revelation 3:11 (KJV), "Behold, I come quickly; hold that fast which thou hast, that no man take thy crown." Christ is telling the believer to persevere. Hold fast to your faith, the truth, the strength of grace, your zeal, and your love for the brethren. Do not let anything or anyone take away your crown. *Behold, I come quickly.* I am coming to relieve them that are under the trial; to reward their fidelity; and to punish those who fall away.

---

[26] Ibid., volume 6 of 6 volumes, pp. 781–782. The crown of life is given to those who endure trials and temptations.

They shall lose that crown which they once seemed to have a right to, which they hoped for, and pleased themselves with thoughts of.[27]

As a believer in Christ Jesus, not only will you get to spend eternity with him because of your faithful service to him, you will receive your crown(s).

"Be thou faithful unto death, and I will give thee a crown of life" was frequently inscribed by early Christians who were persecuted for their faith on the walls of the catacombs in Rome.

---

[27] Ibid., volume 6 of 6 volumes, pp. 914. Hold on to your crown(s) and do not let anything or anyone take it from you.

Dr. Tony Evans's Sermon

"It Is Finished"

On the cross there are seven last sayings, and they are called the seven last statements. We will look at the sixth statement Jesus made, and its recorded in John 19:30 (NKJV). The sixth statement says, "It is finished." In the English language you see three words: it is finished. In the Greek text the New Testament was written in koine, and that's a common language for Greek. It is finished is one word in Greek, and that word is *tetelestai*. This word was used as a regular part of communication during those days. The word *tetelestai* meant the completion of a transaction. Whatever the agreement was has been finally fulfilled or completed. It was always a happy word, and it was used as a victorious word or achievement. When the apostle Paul was lying on his deathbed, he saw that heaven was around the corner. It was a word of achievement and victory. Paul said in 2 Timothy 4:7 (NKJV), "I have fought the good fight, I have finished the race, I have kept the faith." When Jesus said, "it is finished," he was speaking about a task that was victoriously, successfully, and completely finished. It was a word of achievement and victory.

There are four things that come out of this word. The first question is what was finished? Jesus didn't say that he was finished. He was just getting started. What exactly was paid for completely and fully? The issue of the cross involves addressing the problem of sin. The cross is more than an example of sacrifice, more than a simple statement to be made. It has to do with the debt incurred by sin. The human race incurred a debt by sin that it was unable to pay. Have you ever had a debt that you couldn't pay? You've been paying on it for years, and it won't go away. You probably had to refinance it. Why is sin a debt that we can't pay? The reason is because the one who we owe is perfect. All the payments that you make to get rid of the debt can never be repaid because you can't pay your way back into perfection. Most people don't believe it. They believe that the debt of sin, given enough time, religion, going to church, and enough of this and that, can pay off this debt that's owed to a holy God.

Some people don't understand the fundamental principle. God doesn't grade on a curve. You remember going to school, trying to do the best you could, and dying for the teacher to curve the grade. That meant pulling all the scores of all the students, finding out what the average is, and using the average as the high score, which automatically elevates you. Do you remember the nerd in the classroom who always scored one hundred? The nerd's score would mess up the curve. God doesn't grade on a curve, and he doesn't reduce the debt because his nature is perfect.

Something had to address the debt of sin incurred by mankind. Why did Jesus have to say it is finished? Up until he died on the cross it wasn't finished. People were paying on this debt ever since Adam blew it in the Garden of Eden. Lambs were being brought to the altar to put something on this debt. All the lambs did was delay foreclosure. Has anybody ever paid their bills just in the nick of time? Just before the lights go out, or the gas is cut off, or the furniture is put out on the street. Up until Jesus died, they functioned on the layaway plan.

The second principle is what was the payment? It was the death of Christ. It was after he said, "It is finished," that he gave up his spirit and died. Physical death is the separation of the soul from the body, and spiritual death is the separation of the soul from God. While we own the debt, only God has enough to pick up the charge. It's our bill, not God's bill. The only problem with this bill is that you and I don't have what it takes to pick up the tab. Sin is our problem alone, but only God can pay it. If the penalty for sin is death and all of us have sinned, but none of us can pay the tab, how can the tab be paid by God who cannot die since he is a spirit? The answer is God must become a man. It's called the incarnation. The incarnation is where God the Father fertilized the egg of Mary, a human mother. What was born in Bethlehem was the God-man. He was fully God, and God was his Father. He was fully human because Mary was his mother. He was able to die as a man, but have the perfection of God. How was God going to pull this off? *I am going to become just like you. But I am still going to be me. I am going to be the God-man.*

On the cross Jesus Christ fully paid the debt for the sins of men, which required death. On the cross he took the penalty, so he could love the sinner, pay for the sin, satisfy the wrath, and express his love without compromising his nature and his perfection. That's why it was important for Christ to prove he was sinless. But since he was perfect, he could incur your debt for you, for he had no debt of his own. It says in 2 Corinthians 5:21 (NKJV), "For he made him who knew no sin to be sin for us, that we might become the righteousness of God in him." Jesus lived thirty-three years perfectly. He became the substitute for the sins of every man, woman, child, boy, or girl—whoever has been or will be born.

Let me explain how this works. You have one hundred thousand dollars' worth of debt. Bills you cannot pay. Somebody calls you up and tell you that another person has credited your bank account one hundred thousand dollars. This is a credit that was removed from their abundance to your lack of abundance. They take from themself and give to you because you can't pay it. On the cross two things happened. First, Jesus Christ paid the price for your sin which is debt (physically and spiritually). Second, when a person accepts Christ, God takes the thirty-three years of Jesus's perfected life and he credits that to your account. That not only means that you're not in debt, but you have a perfect surplus. He removes your sin and he credits the righteousness to your account. The debt of Christ is the only form of payment that God accepts.

The third point is the proof of the debt. When you go and pay for something, you want proof that payment was made and accepted. When you go to a restaurant they give you the yellow copy, and the white copy is theirs. The white copy says payment was made, and the yellow copy says you can prove it. You can prove that the white copy was given because you possess the yellow copy, and they both say the same thing. It's a receipt. How do we know that we didn't make a mistake banking it all on Christ? How do we know that it ought to be Mohammad, or Buddha, or our own religion? How do we know that the payment was paid in full is predicated on the resurrection? It's the resurrection that places Jesus Christ in a class all by himself. Paul says if the resurrection isn't true, we are still in our sins. Which means the cross without the resurrection is a waste of time. To celebrate Jesus dying and not believe that he rose is ridiculous. Paul says in 1 Corinthians 15:19 (NKJV), "If in this life only we have hope in Christ, we are all men the most pitiable."

Let's go back to the resurrection. Peter and John were told that the stone had been removed from the entrance of Jesus's tomb. They went running, and John outran Peter and reached the tomb first. John stooped down, but he didn't enter the tomb. Finally, Peter arrived and he went inside the tomb, and he saw the turban that had been wrapped around Jesus's head was not lying with the linen cloths, but folded together in a place by itself. When Jesus died on the cross, he had a linen cloth wrapped around his loins and a turban wrapped around his head. When John went into the tomb, he saw the same thing, and he didn't see Jesus there. When he saw that, he knew that Jesus had rose right though his clothes, and now he is alive. At that very moment John said, I believe.

The resurrection is one of the most attested events in human history. If you believe what other historians say about history and you were not there, then you should believe what the Bible says about God and his word. The Bible is the most accurate history book in all of creation, and the resurrection is the testament. It's a receipt that Jesus died on the cross and rose from the grave with all authority and power in his hand.

Between Friday and Sunday, all kinds of things happened. On Good Saturday, Jesus descended into the lower parts of the earth, and when he ascended, he led a host of captives and gave gifts (Ephesians 4:8–10 NKJV). Jesus reached back to the Old Testament saints operating on the layaway plan. He went down to Abraham and Moses and said paid in full. He went back to the all the Old Testament saints who still had not gone to heaven because the final payment hadn't been paid. When stuff is on layaway, you cannot take it out until final payment is made. But when final payment was made, he went back to all the Old Testament saints and he led a host of captives. How do we know that he did that between Friday and Sunday? Jesus Christ on the cross looked at the thief on his right and said today you shall be with me in Paradise. Not on Sunday when I get up, but we are going right now. The resurrection is your receipt.

What do you do with this? Jesus said it is finished, and when John saw it, he said I believe. Sin is a debt you cannot pay. God will not credit your account until you declare bankruptcy. When folks declare bankruptcy, it's when they determine they have a debt that they cannot pay. You declare

JESUS SAID IT'S DONE (WHEN YOUR TIME IS UP)

bankruptcy when all hope is lost to forever liquidate yourself out of this dilemma, and you throw in the towel and you say, "There is absolutely no way I can pay this debt. I'm going to declare Chapter 7 or Chapter 11 (depending on the kind of bankruptcy). I cannot pay it." As long as you think you can he will not credit your account because you think you can do it without him. Because of what Jesus did on the cross, the debt has been paid in full.[28]

---

[28] Dr. Tony Evans, Sermon. It is Finished

It's Time to Make that Change

I love sharing the good news of the gospel, and what God has done for me. Sometimes when my brother saw me coming, he would say, "Here comes John the Baptist." Who is this man? He was the forerunner of Jesus, whose way he was sent to prepare; and he was the one who was crying in the wilderness saying, "Repent, for the Kingdom of heaven is at hand" (Matthew 3:2 NKJV). This message still stands true today. It says in Romans 3:23 (NKJV), "For all have sinned and fall short of the glory of God." The Bible tells us that we need to examine ourselves to see if there is any wickedness in us. The only time some people examine themselves is when they stand in front of a mirror, and that is only to enhance and change their outward appearance. Some are standing too close to the mirror, and the only thing they see is themselves in the natural. Oftentimes they will miss out on seeing the bigger picture, the supernatural, and all the good things that God is doing in their life. It may look good on the outside, but the change that God wants to create starts on the inside of you.

When we sin, we are to repent and ask our heavenly Father in Jesus's name to forgive us of our sin. The Bible says God will forgive us of our sins and remember them no more (Jeremiah 31:34). We also have to forgive one another. When we say the Lord's Prayer, we ask our heavenly Father to forgive us our trespasses (our wrongdoings), as we forgive those who trespass against (wronged) us (Matthew 6:12, 14, 15 NKJV). If we are not willing to forgive those who trespass against us, then our heavenly Father isn't going to forgive us of our sins. We can see the wrongdoings in others, but we have a tendency to overlook ours. It says in Matthew 7:3 (NKJV), "And why do you look at the speck in your brother's eye, but do not consider the plank in your own eye?" Ask God to do this: "Search me, O God, and know my heart; try me and know my anxieties. And see if there is any wicked way in me. And lead me in the way everlasting" (Psalm 139:23–24).

When it comes to your salvation, you cannot save yourself. Jesus is the only one who can save you. Neither is there salvation in any other. There is no other name under heaven given among men whereby you must be saved (Acts 4:12 NKJV). Salvation is given, but there is a condition. If you are not saved, you must repent (ask for forgiveness) of your sins and accept Jesus Christ as your Lord and Savior. God is trying to tell you something—if not now, when? It says in Philippians 2:9–11 (NKJV),

> Therefore God also has highly exalted him and given him the name which is above every name. That at the name of Jesus every knee shall bow of those in heaven, and of those on earth and on those under the earth. And that every tongue

should confess that Jesus Christ is Lord, to the glory of God the Father.

It says in Acts 17:26–28 (NIV),

> From one man he made every nation of men, that they should inhabit the whole earth; and he determined the times set for them and the exact places where they should live. God did this so that men would seek him and perhaps reach out for him and find him, though he is not far from each one of us. For in him we live and move and have our being.

All of creation should be in subjection to him because he is the one and only true living God. There is no one in this world (past, present, or future) who can do what Jesus has done, what he is doing, and what he is going to do. If you don't want to pay homage to him now and voluntarily, there will come a time when you will do it mandatorily.

Time isn't on your side. Look at all the things that are happening around you and the impact that they have had or are having on you, your family, and others around the world. We are here one minute and gone the next. It says in Isaiah 55:6–7 (NKJV), "Seek the Lord while he may be found. Call upon him while he is near. Let the wicked forsake his way. And the unrighteous man his thoughts. Let him return to the Lord. And he will have mercy on him. And to our God, for he will abundantly pardon." I

JESUS SAID IT'S DONE (WHEN YOUR TIME IS UP)

love this quote: "Every saint has a past, and every sinner has a future." God is love. He loves the sinner, but he hates the sin. God still hears a sinner's prayer. This is a short and sweet sinner's prayer:

> Heavenly Father, I confess that I am a sinner, and I have sinned against you. I ask you to forgive me for all my sins. I believe in Jesus's death, burial, and resurrection and that he died on the cross for my sins. I accept Jesus Christ into my life, and I need him to help me to become who he has created me to be. Amen. You must take the necessary steps to find him, and repent for your sins. It says in 2 Peter 3:9 (NIV), "The Lord is not slow in keeping his promise, as some understand slowness. He is patient with you, not wanting anyone to perish, but to come to repentance."

In Luke 23:32–44 we are told about what happened at the crucifixion and the two criminals who were led out with Jesus to be executed. One criminal was on the right of Jesus, and the other on the left. The rulers and the people stood by, watching, and some were hurling insults and mocking Jesus. They said to him, "If you are the Christ of God, the Chosen One, if you are the King of the Jews, save yourself."

One of the criminals joined in with the others in hurling insults at Jesus: "If you are the Christ, save yourself and us."

The other criminal rebuked him and said, "Don't you fear God? He has done nothing wrong. We are the ones who are being punished justly for what we have done."

One of the criminals didn't recognize who Jesus was, and the other one who did said to Jesus, "Remember me when you come into your kingdom."

And Jesus responded, "I tell you the truth. Today you will be with me in paradise."

The unrepentant criminal failed to come to grips with his own sinfulness, and he had no fear of the Lord. He only wanted to be delivered from his current situation. On the other hand, the criminal with the repentant heart confessed his sinfulness and realized that he needed a Savior and Jesus as his Mediator.

Salvation comes when we put our complete faith in Jesus Christ alone. On that day, his physical body died, and his spirit and soul went to paradise with Jesus. And he is waiting for the time where his body will be resurrected.

Jesus said in his word that he came back to save the lost and for them to know the truth. His desire is that none should perish, but have everlasting life with him. The duties required. Seek him and inquire after him as your portion of happiness; seek to be reconciled to him and acquainted with him and to be happy in his favor. Be sorry that you have lost him; be solicitous to find him; take the appointed method of finding him, making use of Christ as your way, the Spirit as your guide, the Word as your rule.

Call upon him. Pray to him to be reconciled, and being reconciled, pray to him for everything else you have need of. The motives are made use of to press these duties upon us: *While he may be found—while he is near.* It is implied that now God is near and will be found so that it shall not be in vain to seek him and to call upon him. Now his patience is waiting on us, his word is calling to us, and his Spirit striving with us. Let us now improve our advantages and opportunities; for now is the accepted time. But there is a day coming when he will be afar off and will not be found when the day of his patience is over, and his Spirit will strive no more. There may come such a time in life when the heart is incurably hardened, and it's certain that at death and judgment the door will be shut (Luke 16:26; 13:25, 26). Mercy is now offered, but then judgment without mercy will take place.[29]

It says in Revelation 3:20 (NKJV), "Behold, I stand at the door and knock. If anyone hears my voice and opens the door, I will come in to him and dine with him, and he with me." He is not going to kick the door in, or use some type of heavy object to bust the door down. He wants you to open the door (your heart) from the inside and let in him. He wants to meet you and have an intimate conversation with you. When you come as you are, Jesus will meet you where you are. He is knocking at the door of your heart—will you let him in? Jesus wants to come in, and take the stony heart out of the flesh, and give you a heart of flesh (Ezekiel 11:19 NKJV). A heart that is kind, loving, forgiving, and willing. God wants to give you a heart that

---

[29] Matthew Henry's *Commentary on the Whole Bible.* New Modern Edition, complete and unabridged in six volumes. Ninth Edition (2009). Peabody, Massachusetts. Hendrickson Publishers Inc. (1991). *Isaiah to Malachi*, volume 4 of 6 volumes, pp. 251. Seek God now while he may be found and while he is near.

will love and serve him and others. A heart that is willing to give. A heart that is willing to praise and worship him.

Are you tired of being sick and tired? When you keep on getting the same unfavorable results, it's time to try something different. It's time to try something new and refreshing. It's time to let go and let God. If you are ashamed of Jesus, he will be ashamed of you. Jesus says in Mark 8:38 (NKJV), "For whoever is ashamed of Me and My words in this adulterous and sinful generation, of him the Son of Man also will be ashamed when he comes in the glory of his Father with the holy angels."

It says in Matthew 6:24 (NKJV), "No one can serve two masters, for either he will hate the one and love the other, or else he will be loyal to the one and despise the other. You cannot serve God and mammon." An idol is any person, place, or thing. The cell phone, social media, title, bank account, job, material wealth, and possessions have become an idol to many. The worldly things that requires most of your time and attention becomes your idol. You can't love the things of the world and serve God too. It says in Exodus 20:3–5 (NKJV),

> You shall have no other gods before me. You shall not make for yourself a carved image—any likeness of anything that is in heaven above, or that is in the earth beneath, or that is in the water under the earth. You shall not bow down to them nor serve them. For I the LORD your God, am a jealous God, visiting the iniquity of the

fathers upon the children to the third and
fourth generations of those who hate me.

In order for you to experience the gift of eternal life, you must receive, trust, and place your confidence and dependence in Jesus Christ. You must entrust your life and your eternal destiny into his hands. If you have not accepted Jesus Christ as your Lord and Savior, you are going be eternally separated from him.

The reason you are still here is because God isn't finished with you yet. Before your time is up, you need to look at your own life and think about your own mortality. Are you living a life that is pleasing unto the Lord? Who will you serve—God, your idol, or the devil? Where will you spend eternity—in heaven or in hell? God is love and he doesn't force you to do anything. He gives you a choice. So you decide. The word of God said:

> For what will it profit a man if he
> gains the whole world and loses his own
> soul. (Mark 8:36 NKJV)

Sometimes there is an ulterior motive behind what mankind does, and it's not always good, but everything God does is good and it's out of love. There is power in his name, in his blood, in his death, in his burial, in his resurrection, in his ascension, and in his Spirit.

If God asked you why should he let you into heaven, what would you say?

My Testimony

It says in Philippians 4:7 (NKJV), "And the peace of God, which surpasses all understanding, will guard your hearts and minds through Christ Jesus." He is called Jehovah Shalom (the Lord our peace).

When I got the call that my brother had transitioned, I notified my family. I stayed up for a while, but I didn't break down. I kept looking at my brother's picture, and I held it close to my heart. I thought I would be torn up from the floor up. I wanted to cry like a baby, but the peace of God would not let it happen. While all hell was breaking loose around me concerning my brother's funeral, God kept me close to his heart and under his wings. And he gently whispered to me and said, *I will never leave you or forsake you.* If I had not held on to his unchanging hands, I probably would have been emotionally distraught and consumed with grief.

Jesus is my Prince of Peace, and when I abide in his presence he brings peace to my heart and soul. I knew I had to cling to the One who can give me the peace that surpasses all understanding. Through his peace and over time, he is strengthening my body, calming my thoughts, healing my heart, and clearing my mind.

I've learned so much during the course of studying God's word about being asleep in him. God is using various aspects of my life—the good, bad, ugly, painful, sorrowful, grief, and passion—for his glory and my spiritual growth and maturity. It is helping me to discover my spiritual gifts and the calling that he has on my life. In my walk with him, I've also learned that he doesn't call the equipped; he equips the called. He is preparing and equipping me for such a time as this, and I look forward to God using me do greater things in his name and for his kingdom.

I do miss my brother a lot, and there is not a day that goes by that I don't think about him. Although, the contact is not there, and he is not here physically, I know for sure that he is in heaven with the Lord. I am being prayerful and hopeful that I will get to see him and my other loved ones again. I thank God from the depth of my heart for giving me his peace, and I give him all the honor, glory, and praise. To God be all the glory for all the good things that he has done!

To all the readers, I pray that this book has blessed, encouraged, and inspired you.

What the Word of God Says

(Scriptures About Death)

Scriptures About Death

The scriptures listed below are to remind us of what the Bible says about death:

> Naked I came from my mother's womb. And naked shall I return there. The LORD gave, and the LORD has taken away. Blessed be the name of the LORD. (Job 1:21 NKJV)

> For I know that my Redeemer lives. And he shall stand at last on the earth. And after my skin is destroyed, this I know. That in my flesh I shall see God. Whom I shall see for myself. And my eyes shall behold, and not another. How my heart yearns within me. (Job 19:25–27 NKJV)

> Most assuredly, I say to you, he who hears my word and believes in him who

sent me has everlasting life, and shall not come to judgment, but has passed from death into life. (John 5:24 NKJV)

I am the resurrection and the life. He who believes in me, though he may die; he shall live. And whoever lives and believes in me shall never die. Do you believe this? (John 11:25–26 NKJV)

We are confident, yes well pleased rather to be absent from the body and to be present with the Lord. (2 Corinthians 5:8 NKJV)

For we brought nothing into this world, and it is certain we can carry nothing out. (1 Timothy 6:7 NKJV)

A good name is better than precious ointment, and the day of death than the day of one's birth. (Ecclesiastes 7:1 NKJV)

Then the dust will return to the earth as it was. And the spirit will return to God who gave it. (Ecclesiastes 12:7 NKJV)

Precious in the sight of the Lord is the death of his saints. (Psalm 116:15 (NKJV)

And do not fear those who kill the body, but cannot kill the soul. But rather fear Him who is able to destroy both soul and body in hell. (Matthew 10:28 NKJV)

For the wages of sin is death, but the gift of God is eternal life in Christ Jesus our Lord. (Romans 6:23 NKJV)

For if we live, we live to the Lord; and if we die, we die to the Lord. Therefore, whether we live or die, we are the Lord's. (Romans 14:8 NKJV)

And as it is appointed for men to die once, but after this judgment. (Hebrews 9:27 NKJV)

What the Word of God Says
(Comforting Scriptures)

Comforting Scriptures

The scriptures below will help to comfort us during our times of sorrow, pain, grief, and trials and tribulations:

> The LORD will give strength to his people. The LORD will bless his people with peace. (Psalm 29:11 NKJV)

> Hear my prayer, O LORD, and give ear to my cry. Do not be silent at my tears; for I am a stranger with you. A sojourner as all my fathers were. Remove your gaze from me that I may regain strength, before I go away and am no more. (Psalm 39:12–13 NKJV)

> Lord, you have been our dwelling place in all generations. Before the mountains were brought forth or ever you had formed the earth and the world. Even

from everlasting to everlasting, you are God. (Psalm 90:1–2 NKJV)

The Lord is my Shepherd; I shall not want. He makes me to lie down in green pastures; he leads me beside the still waters. He restores my soul; he leads me in the paths of righteousness for his name's sake. Yea though I walk through the valley of the shadow of death, I will fear no evil for you are with me; your rod and your staff, they comfort me. You prepare a table before me in the presence of my enemies; you anoint my head with oil; my cup runs over. Surely goodness and mercy shall follow me all the days of my life. And I will dwell in the house of the LORD forever. (Psalm 23:1–6 NKJV)

For God so loved the world that he gave his only begotten Son, that whoever believes in him should not perish but have everlasting life. (John 3:16 NKJV)

God is our refuge and strength. A very present help in trouble. (Psalm 46:1 NKJV)

In the multitude of my anxieties within me your comforts delight my soul. (Psalm 94:19 NKJV)

Blessed are those who mourn. For they shall be comforted. (Matthew 5:4 NKJV)

Let, I pray, your merciful kindness be for my comfort. According to Your word to your servant. Let your tender mercies come to me that I may live. (Psalm 119:76–77 NKJV)

I, even I am he who comforts you. Who are you that you should be afraid. (Isaiah 51:12 NKJV)

Peace I leave with you, my peace I give to you; not as the world gives do I give to you. Let not your heart be troubled, neither let it be afraid. (John 14:27 NKJV)

Who comforts us in all our tribulation that we may be able to comfort those who are in any trouble, with the comfort with which we ourselves are comforted by God? (2 Corinthians 1:4 NKJV)

And let us not grow weary while doing good, for in due season we shall reap if we do not lose heart. (Galatians 6:9 NKJV)

And the peace of God, which surpasses all understanding, will guard your hearts and minds through Christ Jesus. (Philippians 4:7 NKJV)

For since by man came death, by Man also came the resurrection of the dead. For as in Adam all die, even so in Christ all shall be made alive. (1 Corinthians 15:21–22 NKJV)

My flesh and my heart may fail, but God is the strength of my heart and my portion forever. (Psalm 73:26 NKJV)

Therefore you now have sorrow; but I will see you again and your heart will rejoice, and your joy no one will take from you. (John 16:22 NKJV)

I can do all things through Christ who strengthens me. (Philippians 4:13 NKJV)

For I am persuaded that neither death nor life, no angels nor principalities, nor powers, nor things present nor things to come, nor height nor depth, nor any other created thing shall be able to separate us from the love of God which is in Christ Jesus our Lord. (Romans 8:38–39 NKJV)

> Then I heard a voice from heaven saying to me, Write: Blessed are the dead who die in the Lord from now on. Yes, says the Spirit that they may rest from their labors, and their works follow them. (Revelation 14:13 NKJV)

Prayers

(Comforting Prayers)

Comforting Prayers

When we pray the effective and fervent prayer of faith, God hears us. These prayers were written to comfort, uplift, and encourage the family and others. This is one of the comforting prayers that I would give to the grieving family.

> Heavenly Father, in the precious name of your Son, Jesus Christ, and by your Holy Spirit, because of who you are, we give you all the honor, glory, and praise. We exalt, magnify, bless, and glorify your holy name. Your name is above every name, and a power that is above all power.
>
> During this time of bereavement, we thank you for being with the family and friends as they go through their grieving process. Your inspired word said in 1 Thessalonians 4:15–18 (NKJV), "For this we say to you by the word of the Lord,

that we who are alive and remain until the coming of the Lord will by no means precede those who are asleep. For the Lord himself will descend from heaven with a shout, with the voice of an archangel, and with the trumpet of God. And the dead in Christ will rise first. Then we who are alive and remain shall be caught up together with them in the clouds to meet the Lord in the air. And thus we shall always be with the Lord. Therefore comfort one another with these words."

Heavenly Father, we thank you for the life of our beloved, and we know that in our Father's house a special place is being prepared for our loved one.

Your word reminds us that to everything there is a season, and time to every purpose under the heaven. There is a time to be born and a time to die. There is a time to weep, and a time to laugh, a time to mourn, and a time to dance. For all those who are grieving, know that you have been assured by God's word that blessed are they that mourn, for they shall be comforted; and that weeping may endure for a night, but joy will come.

Heavenly Father, in the holy and marvelous name of Jesus, and by your Spirit, by your *dunamis* power, and by your infinite wisdom, we ask that you will:

> encourage and strengthen the family,
> give them peace that surpasses all understanding,
> let your unfailing agape love comfort and protect them,
> heal and restore their broken hearts, and
> show them your continued faithfulness, compassion, tender mercies, lead, and guide them each day and every step of the way.
> As time moves forward, we pray that you will give the family:
> beauty for ashes,
> the oil of joy for mourning, and
> the garment of praise for a spirit of heaviness.

We speak life, favor, blessing, and your fresh anointing over the entire family. We pray that: "The Lord will bless and keep them. May the Lord shine his face upon them and be gracious unto them. May the Lord lift up his countenance and give them peace that surpasses all understanding. May the Lord bless their children and their children's children" (Numbers 6:24–27 NKJV).

We pray that the sweet memories of your beloved will be a blessing to the family.

In the mighty name of Jesus Christ, we pray. Amen.

Heavenly Father, I know that death will eventually come to all of us. Lord, oftentimes it is so hard to say goodbye and to give up my beloved. I know that my loved one will go to a better place, but my grief and pain overwhelm me. I ask that you comfort me during these times and fill this empty void with your peace and joy. Strengthen me on every side and give me what I need to make it through each day. Teach me how to number my days and order my steps in your word.

In the wonderful name of Jesus, I pray. Amen.

Heavenly Father, I thank you for your loving kindness and faithfulness toward me doing my grieving process. You said in your word that you will never leave me or forsake me and you will keep me in the palm of your righteous right hand. I thank you for encamping your angels around me, and for being my refuge and my rock doing these painful times in my life. I thank you for healing and restoring my soul and for showering me with your *agape* love, grace, and tender mercies.

In the matchless name of Jesus, I pray. Amen.

Heavenly Father, your word tells me not to become weary because you are with me, and not to be afraid because you are my God. That you will strengthen and uplift me. Although the storms may come and the winds may blow, I will remain steadfast and hold on to your unchanging hands. I put my hope and trust in you because you have been my anchor and my firm foundation, and I know that you will never let me down. Give me the peace that surpasses all understanding and the willingness to meet each day with gladness. Give me a faith that is bigger than my feelings. Help me not to focus on the challenges and the circumstances, but to keep my focus on you.

In the blessed name of Jesus, I pray. Amen.

Heavenly Father, I thank you for being a God of love and mercy. What is impossible with man is possible with you. You are the same God who never fails, and I know that you won't fail me now and that you are working all things out for my good. Although life can leave some scars, you are the balm of Gilead who can heal all my wounds and fix what is broken. I thank you for your faithfulness toward me and for helping me to stand on your word and your promises.

In the powerful name of Jesus, I pray. Amen.

Heavenly Father, I thank you for being my rock and refuge, and that I can abide under the shadow of the Almighty because you are my God, and in you will I trust. Because you live, I know I can face tomorrow without any fear or doubt. Throughout life's challenges, I've seen the evidence of your goodness all over my life and the fulfillment of your promises. I thank you for all the blessing and favor that you have bestowed upon me even when I didn't deserve them. Wherever I find myself in this life, I will give you all the honor, glory, and praise because I know that I serve an awesome God who loves me unconditionally. I will trust in your name to do great things in my life.

In the sacred name of Jesus, I pray. Amen.

Poems
(Thoughts and Expressions)

To Our Beloved Dre

Although we've shed many heartaches, pains, and tears, we knew that our faith in God was not based on how we feel. Through it all, we knew that God's *agape* love and faithfulness are always real.

He saw your weakness, struggles, and pains; and the life that you lived on this earth will not go unnoticed. And it wasn't lived in vain.

In your darkest days and nights, God said in his word that he would make it all right. And during those times he continued to love and strengthen you with all his might.

Our beloved Dre, you touched our lives in so many ways. You blessed us with your love, kindness, and laughter day after day. Your presence was a blessing and felt in so many ways.

Deep in our heart, we know that God doesn't make a mistake or fail. And in the end, his plan for your life prevailed.

Our beloved Dre, although we wanted you to stay, God's thoughts and ways are always best. He gave you your angelic wings, and he called you home to eternal rest.

Although you aren't with us physically, we know that you will always be with us spiritually. Our love toward you will always be embedded in our heart, and nothing will ever separate us or keep us apart.

Rebecca Griffin

Jesus Said It's Done

When your breathing became shallow and your body began to shut down, Jesus surrounded you with his angels and said I look forward to giving you your crown.

When your pain and suffering became too much for you to bear, Jesus said, I Am the Greatest Physician, and now you are under my care.

When the heaven opened up and Jesus received you unto himself, he said welcome home, My beloved, don't be concerned about them or the things that were left.

When all the doctors gave up and said there was no medical cure, God said when the time comes, your old corruptible body will become pure.

When man's ways failed, Jesus purpose and plan for your life prevailed. He took complete charge over your life because he is a God who can do anything but fail.

When the days and nights became so fretful and weary. Jesus said, "The new life that I have planned for you will not be unforgettable or dreary."

When the storms came and the winds blew, you tried to remain steadfast, but God whispered in your ear and said even this, too, shall pass.

Rebecca Griffin

Irreplaceable

You were a bright shining star that separated you from all the rest. But God knew what he was doing when he gave us the best.

We laughed, cried, and prayed together, and remembered the days of old. But God reminded us that you are worth more than silver and gold.

Although you are gone away from our sight; we will always remember you as our bright shining light who gave all that you had within your might.

While you were here with us you were such a rare essence, and as each day goes by, we will truly miss your presence.

As we watched you slip away like a ship passing in the midst of a fog, God graciously stepped in and lowered his anchor and said, "Well done." Welcome aboard.

Rest well, our beloved, until we meet again. Because of who God is, we know that he still sits on his throne and he rules and reigns.

Rebecca Griffin

Gone but Not Forgotten

Although you are gone, our hearts are heavy, and our eyes well up with tears; it's because we have lost someone who was so precious and dear.

Although you are gone, no one can ever take your place, but we look forward to that day when we will see you again face-to-face.

Although you are gone, life with you as we knew it will never be the same, but our unwavering love for you will always remain.

Although you are gone, we go back to revisit the past because we want all the good memories that are embedded in our heart of you to last.

Although you are gone, your laughter and smile will be truly missed, but we know that your soul belongs to the Lord and will still exist.

Although you are gone, we know that you are being taken care of by the best, because God is the One who called you home to eternal rest.

Rebecca Griffin

God Knows Best

Even in your sickness, pain, and affliction, we wanted you to stay. But we were reminded of our selfishness if we wanted to continue seeing you that way.

It was painful and heart-wrenching to see you in this state. But we know that he is an on-time God and he never makes a mistake or shows up late.

Sometimes it's hard to say goodbye to yesterday. But we are reminded that he is the same God yesterday and today.

In this life, we were hoping and praying for a miraculous cure that wasn't meant to be. And God graciously and mercifully stepped in and said, "My beloved, come and go with Me."

God knew that your time was getting near, and he gently reminded you to sleep peacefully in him and to have no regret or fear.

Life and death are always in the power of his hands because abundant life and eternal life are a part of his purpose and plan.

God reminds us not to become so overwhelmed in our tears and grief, but remember that I Am the Great I Am who will always be there to comfort us and give us relief.

Rebecca Griffin

Releasing You Back to God

We release our beloved soul back to you because in due time the old body will become brand-new. All the worldly things will be seen from a heavenly point of view.

We release our beloved back to you because this is where you are destined to be. There is no other God who has a better purpose and plan for you and me.

We release all your suffering, heartache, and pain, and when you receive your new resurrected body, you will have everything to gain.

We release our beloved because you were called by name. We release you back to the Creator from whence you came.

We release that void of our loss that pierced our heart. And we know deep down inside that nothing will ever separate or keep us apart.

We release you like a dove that has left the nest. But we know deep down in our heart that you are surrounded by the best.

Rebecca Griffin

My Heavenly Home

Before Jesus ascended into heaven, he said he was going away to prepare a place for me, and that where he is, also I am to be.

The new place that I am going to now sits eternally in the heavens where Jesus sits upon his throne, he said you are now in my presence, and you will never be left alone.

This heavenly place that I am going to will be nothing like what I have ever seen; Jesus has prepared this place for me, and it's described as beautiful and serene.

This heavenly place is where Jesus will always rule and reign; there is plenty of room for all those he wants to welcome and receive in his name.

I was a foreigner who once lived in a strange land; he welcomed me home so I could be included in his master plan.

Rebecca Griffin

Jesus Set Me Free

Jesus set me free from all my suffering, pain, and misery; he said to be absent from the body is to be present with Me.

Jesus set me free from the world and all its strife because he is the resurrection and the way, truth, and life.

Jesus set me free because the burden and the yoke were trying to take over me, but the Anointed One told me I will always be with thee.

Jesus set me free when all else was beyond man's finite capabilities; he stepped in and said let me show you my infinite power and abilities.

Jesus set me free, and now I am in a peaceful and restful place, where one day soon I will see him and his glory face-to-face.

Rebecca Griffin

Jesus Did It All for Me

What you did on Calvary was not just for me; without your *agape* love, grace, mercy, and faithfulness, where would I be?

You defeated death because you were resurrected from the grave, because of your love and unselfishness you gave and gave.

Because of what you have done, I have the victory, and I look forward to spending eternity with you and being a part of history.

Abundant and eternal life is only found in God's Son because he is my redeemer, the Holy and Anointed One.

You were there with me in the beginning, and you will be there at the end. I will rest peacefully in Jesus until he descends.

When our heavenly Father gave us his only begotten Son, because of him, death has no sting and the victory has already been won.

Rebecca Griffin

God's Masterpiece

His purpose and plan for you are to be who he created you to be; this also includes his plan for your destiny.

You are a rare creation who is different from all the rest; he knew what he was doing when he created the best.

When he created you, he did not stumble, and he didn't make a mistake, and it was all done in love for his glory and name sake.

He has given you a spirit, soul, and a body; this masterpiece wasn't designed and created by just anybody. In his eyes, you are unique and special and looked upon as being somebody.

To him you are deemed so precious and rare; no one on this earth can create what God has done or even compare.

He didn't need a blueprint when he created you out of his love and affection; he saw what he did and marveled at his most beautiful possession.

This masterpiece can't be duplicated because it's one of a kind; before you were conceived in your mother's womb he had you in mind.

Rebecca Griffin

Bibliography

Matthew Henry's *Commentary on the Whole Bible*. New Modern Edition, complete and unabridged in six volumes. Ninth Edition (2009). Peabody, Massachusetts. Hendrickson Publishers Inc. (1991), *Isaiah to Malachi*, volume 4 of 6 volumes, pp. 56. The burden will be lifted, and the yoke will be taken away.

———. *Job to Song of Solomon*, volume 3 of 6 volumes, pp. 819. Everything under heaven (earth) is changeable, but in heaven they are unchangeable.

———. *Job to Song of Solomon*, volume 3 of 6 volumes, pp. 819. A time to be born, a time to die, and a time to rise.

Karnes, Barbara. *Gone from My Sight: The Dying Experience* Vancouver, Washington (1986), revised 2020, pp. 1–13. Various signs of death, but they may or may not apply to everyone.

Matthew Henry's *Commentary on the Whole Bible*. New Modern Edition, complete and unabridged in six volumes. Ninth Edition (2009). Peabody, Massachusetts. Hendrickson Publishers, Inc. (1991), *Genesis to Deuteronomy*, volume 1 of 6 volumes, pp. 40–41. Enoch was translated that he should not see death.

———. *Joshua to Esther*, volume 2 of 6 volumes, pp. 553–555. Elijah was translated that he should not see death.

Evans, Dr. Tony. Sermon. "The Rapture and the Church."

Matthew Henry's *Commentary on the Whole Bible.* New Modern Edition, complete and unabridged in six volumes. Ninth Edition (2009). Peabody, Massachusetts. Hendrickson Publishers Inc. (1991), *Acts to Revelation*, volume 6 of 6 volumes, pp. 598. There is a glory reserved for the bodies of the saints, which they will be instated at the resurrection.

Unger, Merrill F. *Unger's Bible Dictionary*, revised and updated edition (1988). The Moody Bible Institute of Chicago, pp. 178. The Book of Life refers to the roster of righteous who are to inherit eternal life from which the saved are not blotted out.

Matthew Henry's *Commentary on the Whole Bible.* New Modern Edition, complete and unabridged in six volumes. Ninth Edition (2009). Peabody, Massachusetts. Hendrickson Publishers Inc. (1991). *Acts to Revelation*, volume 6 of 6 volumes, pp. 912. I will not blot his name out of the Book of Life, but will confess his name before my Father, and before angels.

Unger, Merrill F. *Unger's Bible Dictionary,* revised and updated edition (1988). The Moody Bible Institute of Chicago, pp. 728. All must appear before the judgment seat of Christ that each one may be recompensed for his deeds in the body according to what he has done.

———. pp. 727. This last great judgment is called the white throne judgment. All who are not found in the Book of Life are cast into the lake of fire.

Alcorn, Randy. *Heaven*. USA: Tyndale House Publishers Inc. "Introduction: The Subject of Heaven." *In Heaven*. xvii. Mr. Alcorn's bibliography: J. Sidlow Baxter, *The Other Side of Death: What the Bible Teaches about Heaven and Hell* (Grand Rapids: Kregel (1987), 237. Harvey Minkoff, *The Book of Heaven* (Owings Mills, Maryland: Ottenheimer, 2001), 87. Edward Donnelly, *Biblical Teaching on the Doctrines of Heaven and Hell* (Edinburgh: Banner of Truth, 2001), 64. Don Richardson, *Eternity in Their Hearts*, rev. ed. (Ventura, California: Regal, 1984). How other civilizations viewed the afterlife:

Baxter, J. Sidlow. Native Americans believed that in the afterlife, their spirits would hunt the spirits of buffalo.

Minkoff, Harvey. In the pyramids of Egypt, the embalmed bodies had maps placed beside them as a guide to the future world.

Donnelly, Edward. The Romans believed that the righteous would picnic in the Elysian Fields while their horses grazed nearby.

Richardson, Don. Anthropological evidence suggests that every culture has a God-given innate sense of the eternal—that this world is not all there is.

Matthew Henry's *Commentary on the Whole Bible*. New Modern Edition, complete and unabridged in six volumes. Ninth Edition (2009). Peabody, Massachusetts. Hendrickson Publishers Inc. (1991). *Acts to Revelation*, volume 6 of 6 volumes, pp. 598. This world is not our home. The believer's citizenship is in heaven, and their conversations should be focused on things that are above.

Merrill F. Unger's bibliography references on the ascension. H. B. Swete, *The Ascended Christ* (1911); C. F. D. Moule, *Expository Times* 68 (1957); 205–9; W. J. Sparrow-Simpson, *Our Lord's Resurrection* (1964); id., *The Resurrection and the Christian* (1968); W. Milligan, *The Ascension of Christ* (1980); P. Toon, *The Ascension of Our Lord* (1984). The ascension of Jesus Christ and the doctrinal and ethical significance.

Merrill F. Unger's bibliography references. E. M. Bounds, *Heaven: A Place, a City, a Home* (1921); W. M. Smith, *The Biblical Doctrine of Heaven* (1968); N. Turner, *Christian Words* (1982), pp. 202–05. Heaven is the abode of the Triune God, a place of beauty, life, service, worship, and glory.

Matthew Henry's *Commentary on the Whole Bible*. New Modern Edition, complete and unabridged in six volumes. Ninth Edition (2009). Peabody, Massachusetts. Hendrickson Publishers Inc (1991). *Acts to Revelation*, volume 6 of 6 volumes, pp. 954-955. The pure river of water, and the fruitful tree of life.

Unger, Merrill F. *Unger's Bible Dictionary*, revised and updated edition (1988). The Moody Bible Institute of Chicago, pp. 1080. God offers the believers rewards based on their faithful service rendered after salvation.

Matthew Henry's *Commentary on the Whole Bible*. New Modern Edition, complete and unabridged. Ninth edition (2009). Peabody, Massachusetts. Hendrickson Publishers Inc. (1991). *Acts to Revelation*, volume 6 of 6 volumes, pp. 445–446. The incorruptible crown is given to the believers who overcome and endure trials and temptations.

———. volume 6 of 6 volumes, pp. 684. The crown of righteousness is the recompense of the believer's service, which God is not unrighteous to forget.

———. volume 6 of 6 volumes, pp. 627. The crown of joy is given to the believers who show mutual love and affection toward each other and rejoice together in the Second Coming of Jesus Christ.

———. volume 6 of 6 volumes, pp. 832–833. The crown of glory is given to the faithful preachers and teachers who feed the flock, are an example of holiness, and carry out their duties as God prescribed.

———. volume 6 of 6 volumes, pp. 781–782. The crown of life is given to those who endure trials and temptations.

———. volume 6 of 6 volumes, pp. 914. Hold on to your crown(s), and do not let anything or anyone take it from you.

Evans, Dr. Tony. Sermon. "It is Finished."

Matthew Henry's *Commentary on the Whole Bible*. New Modern Edition, complete and unabridged in six volumes. Ninth Edition (2009). Peabody, Massachusetts. Hendrickson Publishers Inc. (1991). *Isaiah to Malachi*, volume 4 of 6 volumes, pp. 251. Seek God now while he may be found and while he is near.

About the Author

Rebecca Griffin lives in Prince George's County, Maryland. She has a bachelor's degree in business management. She has served as a deacon, taught several Bible classes, and is currently teaching on the Gospel Train Prayer Line. One of her favorite scriptures is Ephesians 2:10 (NKJV), "For we are His workmanship, created in Christ Jesus for good works, which God prepared beforehand that we should walk in them."

Hearing and studying the word of God and walking with him are helping her to discover who she is, whose she is, and what she has in Christ Jesus. She enjoys reading, helping, serving others, and giving God the glory for all the good things that he has done in her life. This is the first time that she has written a book, and it has helped her tremendously as she goes through her grieving process. And she prays and hopes that her book will be a blessing and a comfort to you.

Printed in the USA
CPSIA information can be obtained
at www.ICGtesting.com
CBHW020950260724
12186CB00038B/311